PRAISE
FIRST EDITION

"Anderson's framework is innovative, and the discussion questions included after each chapter will usefully guide the conversations that this provocative manifesto is sure to inspire."
Publishers Weekly, April 9, 2007

"After reading this book, I am convinced: we need gracism. Division and inequality are consequences of our fallen world. But as the members of the church we must walk against division and injustice. The brilliance of this book is that we are shown how to overcome individual-level racism, clearly and plainly. Dr. Anderson provides us with real tools for real life. Gracism is an act, a state of being. Members of the body, let's be gracists."
Michael Emerson, founding director, Center on Race, Religion, and Urban Life, Rice University, and coauthor of *Divided by Faith* and *United by Faith*

"Dr. David Anderson is one of the finest reconciliation practitioners that I know. In this book, *Gracism: The Art of Inclusion,* he honestly shares his journey into a profound concept that has the potential to revolutionize how we confront racism to create a society with liberty and justice for all."
Brenda Salter McNeil, president, Salter McNeil Associates, LLC, coauthor of *The Heart of Racial Justice: How Soul Change Leads to Social Change*

"Anderson provides us with more than just a theoretical or political rationale for Christians to work toward racial reconciliation. He also provides us with practical methods by which this reconciliation may be achieved. *Gracism* needs to become a term common to Christians of all races. As we follow the advice in this important book we will find ourselves becoming inclusive of those who are different than us. As Anderson so ably demonstrates, it is when we develop the heart and skills necessary for such a conclusion that we will be able to truly adopt Christlike attitudes toward our racially different neighbors and colleagues."
George Yancey, associate professor of sociology, University of North Texas, author of *Beyond Racial Gridlock*

"David Anderson speaks, lives and is called to the truth of multicultural relationships and ministry. This book is not a book just for black people to work with whites or whites to learn how to be sensitive to blacks, but a book about God's practical, real transforming grace for all people to be kingdom people."

Phil Jackson, lead pastor, The House, coauthor, *The Hip-Hop Church*

"David Anderson addresses one of the real solutions to the issue of racism with this difficult practice of grace! David's take from an African American perspective enlightens us to how deep racism runs even in Christian institutions and relationships, but more than that, he also offers us a biblical initiative to lead us to the vision of being a community that reflects the diversity of God."

Dave Gibbons, lead pastor, NewSong Church, and CVO, Xealot Inc.

"A tough-minded book and clear-sighted look at what it means for Christians to 'overcome evil with good.' If metaphor is metamorphosis, the metaphor of 'gracism' will change how we do church like it's changed how I do life."

Leonard Sweet, E. Stanley Jones Professor of Evangelism, The Theological School, Drew University, and visiting distinguished professor, George Fox University

"With profound concepts and a compelling voice, *Gracism* creates an accessible tool for navigating culture clashes. Anderson merges a sophisticated understanding of cultural dynamics with real-time, everyday advice. He takes old-time concepts like 'favor' and gives them flesh and blood for a modern world."

Nikki A. Toyama, coeditor of *More Than Serving Tea: Asian American Women on Expectations, Relationships, Leadership and Faith*

"Dr. David Anderson has given us both a great new word and a fresh way to approach our racial and cultural divisions in the church—and in life. I'm hoping a huge audience will read this book and discover the heart and passion of one of the racial reconciliation movement's most dynamic young leaders."

Edward Gilbreath, author of *Reconciliation Blues: A Black Evangelical's Inside View of White Christianity*

"What a beautiful—and needed!—book. Dave Anderson calls people who are saved by the grace of God to extend grace to their neighbors, whoever they are. I can't imagine anyone reading this book without being marked for life as an agent of gracism, which may be the best synonym for *reconciliation* ever invented."
Brian D. McLaren, author/activist

"David Anderson is a powerful voice of hope and a national leader in racial reconciliation. This book provides a new—and the only— 'ism' that can heal the deep wounds of racism."
Donald T. Floyd Jr., president and CEO, National 4-H Council

GRACISM

THE ART OF INCLUSION

DAVID A. ANDERSON

REVISED AND EXPANDED
WITH DAVID HEILIGER

FOREWORD BY
ERWIN RAPHAEL McMANUS

An imprint of InterVarsity Press
Downers Grove, Illinois

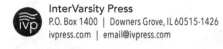

InterVarsity Press
P.O. Box 1400 | Downers Grove, IL 60515-1426
ivpress.com | email@ivpress.com

InterVarsity Press® is the publishing division of InterVarsity Christian Fellowship/USA®. For more information, visit intervarsity.org.

All Scripture quotations, unless otherwise indicated, are taken from The Holy Bible, New International Version®, NIV®. Copyright © 1973, 1978, 1984, 2011 by Biblica, Inc.™ Used by permission of Zondervan. All rights reserved worldwide. www.zondervan.com. The "NIV" and "New International Version" are trademarks registered in the United States Patent and Trademark Office by Biblica, Inc.™

While any stories in this book are true, some names and identifying information may have been changed to protect the privacy of individuals.

The publisher cannot verify the accuracy or functionality of website URLs used in this book beyond the date of publication.

Cover design: David Fassett
Interior design: Jeanna Wiggins

ISBN 978-1-5140-0732-7 (print) | ISBN 978-1-5140-0733-4 (digital)

Printed in the United States of America ♾

Library of Congress Cataloging-in-Publication Data
Names: Anderson, David A., 1966- author. | Heiliger, David, author.
Title: Gracism : the art of inclusion / David A. Anderson ; with David
  Heiliger.
Description: Revised and expanded edition. | Downers Grove, IL :
  InterVarsity Press, 2023. | Includes bibliographical references.
Identifiers: LCCN 2022054205 (print) | LCCN 2022054206 (ebook) | ISBN
  9781514007327 (print) | ISBN 9781514007334 (ebook)
Subjects: LCSH: Church and minorities. | Social integration–Religious
  aspects–Christianity. | Multiculturalism–Religious
  aspects–Christianity. | Marginality, Social–Religious
  aspects–Christianity. | Christianity and culture. |
  Reconciliation–Religious aspects–Christianity.
Classification: LCC BV639.M56 A53 2023 (print) | LCC BV639.M56 (ebook) |
  DDC 241/.675–dc23/eng/20230117
LC record available at https://lccn.loc.gov/2022054205
LC ebook record available at https://lccn.loc.gov/2022054206

29   28   27   26   25   24   23 | 13   12   11   10   9   8   7   6   5   4   3   2   1

CONTENTS

FOREWORD
Erwin Raphael McManus

It was nearly twenty years ago that I first met David Anderson in a room facing Lake Michigan. Among those present were Andy Stanley and Ed Young Jr. Frankly, I thought I was in the room with legends. I really had no idea why I had been invited to such a meeting, but I was honored to be present.

In that meeting, David Anderson was identified as America's critical voice on the issue of racial reconciliation. Even then there was an undeniable divide between not only the church but also the nation when it came to race and our nation's unfortunate past when it came to slavery.

What has transpired across the nation over the past twenty years only makes David's voice more essential.

Bookended by the infamous terrorist act of 9/11 and the global pandemic and quarantine of 2020, recent events in the United States have led us to be in the midst of a cultural crisis around the issues of slavery, race, and justice. From Rodney King to Trayvon Martin, the narratives of social justice, racial equality, and racism remind us that our nation is more divided today than it was twenty years ago.

David's first edition of *Gracism* offered a dramatically different way forward than was being heralded by the cultural experts at the time. He wrote long before the Black Lives Matter movement emerged as a voice calling for justice and restitution.

David spoke to this issue before the contrast of being a Black American and a White American came to the forefront of our collective consciousness, before Colin Kaepernick took a knee, before the narrative of Black Lives Matter captured our social consciousness and opened a cultural wound that had not been healed. There was a clarion call for justice and equality and dignity.

The solutions, though, seem to only offer us a future with more wounds and less healing. As a nation we want to make things right. Yet it seems we do not know how to make them better. How do we heal a nation that has wounded itself?

What David adds—that has been mostly unheard—is that healing cannot happen without grace. He calls us to see that we cannot end racism if we do not elevate to gracism.

This is why, when I joined David at Bridgeway after the pandemic and quarantine came to an end, I encouraged him to rerelease his book. It was ahead of its time, but it is needed in our time more than ever.

David, like the name of your church, you are a bridge between cultures, colors, and communities. May your message of reconciliation be heard far and wide. Thank you for pointing to the way of Jesus and calling us all to follow him toward grace and peace. It's a pleasure to have reconnected in our friendship and our mission.

There can never be too much grace in the world.

INTRODUCTION

Excited about my opportunity to serve as an intern at Willow Creek Community Church in South Barrington, Illinois, I was looking forward to my first day on the job. After three years of Bible education in downtown Chicago at Moody Bible Institute, and two years of urban pastoral ministry in Cabrini Green, a poor black neighborhood replete with high-rise apartments fencing in humans like rats in a cage, I was now about to enter a completely different experience.

As a tall African American male, my new reality as a Willow employee placed me in a suburban context among a sea of white people. This context included beautifully designed mansions and shiny luxury vehicles that occupied multiple garages. The landscaped lawns were works of art religiously primped and usually cared for by Hispanic men who edged and mowed the well-manicured acreage. It was a far cry from the urine-stained elevators and graffiti-ridden projects of Cabrini.

I wasn't raised in either extreme. I didn't come from wealth or poverty. Both of my parents worked full-time jobs outside the home but made it home each night by dinnertime, when we all ate together. Our single-family home was a small brick Cape Cod with three bedrooms, one bathroom, a basement, and a yard surrounded by a chainlink fence. My father worked for the federal government, while my mother worked for the state of Maryland; we four children attended public schools. During my elementary school years, I stayed with a neighborhood daycare provider after school until Mom came home from work.

Heading to Chicago was a big deal for me because I had seldom traveled beyond the Washington metropolitan area. My home metropolis was demographically diverse, and there everyone seemed to work hard to hold down their jobs, pay their mortgages, and protect their families from the social ills of drugs and violence. Once I landed in Chicago, though, the extremes of racial existence were stark. It seemed as if the majority of whites were rich and educated, while the blacks were poor and uneducated. The Hispanics were in their own enclaves and the Asians were seemingly invisible except in Chinatown or Koreatown. For me as a minister in my twenties, my views about diversity, class distinctions, social conditioning, and racial reconciliation were challenging my vision for multicultural ministry amid the extremes of society.

Throughout my life, I had grown up conscious of race and was aware of how the racial issues that plagued our country affected me personally and systemically, but I had never felt as powerless as I did on my first day as an intern at Willow. The day was marked by a set of racially penetrating events now etched in my memory. As I commuted to the church that first morning in my rusted-out, blue Honda Civic, I noticed blue lights flashing in my rearview mirror. A police officer was signaling me to pull over. With my hands in clear view, I gave the officer my license and registration. He went back to his vehicle. I assumed he was checking my information on the computer and doing whatever else police officers do in their cars while the stopped driver sits in embarrassment along the side of the road as motorists pass and gawk.

When the officer returned to my driver's side window, he handed my license to me. I was dismissed.

"Before you leave, sir, can you tell me why I was pulled over?" I asked.

The officer responded, "You fit the description of someone we are looking for."

I took him at his word.

Had that been my only experience of being pulled over that day, I would have believed that the inconvenience of mistaken identity could have happened to anyone. But a few hours later I drove off the church campus to get lunch; again I had the sinking feeling in my stomach that comes with the realization that one is being stopped by a police officer.

"What's wrong now?" I said aloud to myself. *Bad luck indeed,* I thought.

Like it was déjà vu, I went through the same delay that made me late on my first day of work earlier that morning. I received from the second officer the same explanation given to me by the first cop who had stopped me. "You fit the description of someone we are looking for," he said. At this point I thought it would be great if the officers could make a note in their system to let everyone know that David Anderson was not the guy they were looking for! I was upset.

What made the day so memorable was not the orientation to one of the coolest megachurches I had been exposed to at the time or the grace with which the staff greeted me when I was introduced. What was most memorable was that I was tardy on my first day as an intern due to a delay from a police officer. The day is memorable because I was stopped again on my way to lunch. But if that were the end of the story, we could record this scenario as a minor inconvenience that all people in the suburbs of Chicago might have to endure on occasion. Unfortunately, on my way back from lunch, I was stopped by a third officer. Before the day was over, I had been stopped by four police officers. Three were male, one was female, and all were white. I never received a ticket or harsh treatment, thankfully.

Can you imagine the frustration, the anger, and even the self-questioning that were unearthed inside me? Years before this incident, I had become convinced that God had called me to reconciliation and multicultural ministry. I was a minister of the gospel and more importantly a Christ-follower. I cannot imagine the bitter attitudes and negative behaviors that would have come out of me had I not been tempered by the Holy Spirit living inside me at that young age of twenty-three. The Spirit's presence did not relieve me of the deflated feelings I experienced that evening after my first day of work. But as I reflected on the day's events, anger gave way to the comfort of the Holy Spirit. God reiterated in me that this was why my life must be committed to building bridges of reconciliation.

What I experienced that day was racism. What I envision is a world that can move from racism to gracism. *Gracism,* unlike racism, doesn't focus on race for negative purposes such as discrimination. Gracism focuses on race for the purpose of positive ministry and service. When the grace of God can be communicated through the beauty of race, then you have gracism. My prayer is that this book will move God's people closer to achieving such a worthy vision.

1

EVERYONE HAS A DOT

Maybe you have heard of the social experiment in which ten people were to interview at a company. Before they went into the office for the interview, a red dot was painted on one cheek of each interviewee. Each interviewee was to go into the office and sit across the desk from the interviewer. After each interview, the interviewee was debriefed. Each of the ten interviewees stated that the interviewer kept staring at the dot on his or her cheek.

Here is the kicker: Out of the ten who received a painted dot, five—unbeknownst to them—were actually given a clear dot that was not visible on their skin. Yet they still felt as if the interviewer was focusing on their dot. From this experiment we learn that people feel self-conscious about whatever makes them insecure. That insecurity might relate to one's weight, gender, race, or any other distinctive that is viewed as a negative in society. Do you ever feel like people are focusing on your red dot?

When I was pulled over by police officers in the suburbs of Chicago four times within a single day, I knew that my racial dot was bright and noticeable. At first I told myself that I was being self-conscious; I tried to convince myself that race was not the issue. After the second stop, though, I knew that race was the issue whether or not I could ever prove it.

DOTISM

It's no secret that North America used to be notorious around the world for heinous acts of slavery followed by an era of politically legislated and corporate policy-backed racial discrimination and segregation. Racial prejudice was a proud badge of honor for many in the United States in generations past. There was a time when it was widely accepted to publicly declare that only white was right and everything else, from Native American, to African, to Chinese, to Jewish, was wrong. Now many people remain unaware or in denial of the extent to which the embedded effects of our racialized roots are still at work today. For those that boldly stand behind their racially biased or abusive views, they often attempt to veil it so as not to face the consequences of cancel culture. We have seen over the past decade a new era of racial struggle in which previously dormant issues have come to the forefront. And through the channels of social media and commercial news outlets, masses of people are engaging in seemingly twenty-four-hour access to the unrest. Protests, demonstrations, and uprisings have united changemakers while inflaming those who disagree. We have a war of ideologies in which it feels like one side is fighting to protect their lives while the other is fighting to protect their livelihood.

If we look to generations past, by and large (with the help of the sovereign hand of the Almighty) it was the great struggle of blacks for their freedom, with the help of courageous whites and others, that achieved the major advancements of that day. Today we see the same movement—those in the minority are doing whatever it takes to elevate the issues that center on their very dignity, which those in the majority have had the privilege to dismiss.

Because the cycle of racialized conflict is so relentless, racial discussions often feel forced and unsafe. Many feel the extremes: these conversations are either overplayed or underaddressed. The layers of this ongoing conflict have affected not just interpersonal relationships, but even a person's self-identity. When you have groups of people in a country who feel like they have dots on their faces and have been made to feel that their dots are ugly, unwanted, and limiting to their success, you will find corresponding behaviors that contribute to those self-perceptions. Many with dots feel as if they must overachieve in order to succeed in society. What is being revealed is that we have people throughout our country who feel unwanted and disfavored, have no reassurance that their lives matter to the collective, and who are not invited to the table of influence. Racially, those in the minority continue to face barriers to achieving the same financial or career success as their racial counterparts, and often that pathway to success is marked by forced submission, assimilation, and not rocking the boat. The message is clear: You can stay as long as you try to hide your dot and attempt to blend in.

Over decades, many dotted people have been wrongly accused and denied employment, promotions, or housing. Many people have been beaten, jailed, and treated as less than human because of their dots. So after a while, dotted persons understandably recognize that others treat them as though their dottedness is a liability. They can no longer ignore the reality that they are being prejudged based on their facial dot.

REAL LIFE

I had just returned home from consulting for a large corporate client in the heartland of the United States. One of the stories I received from an African American woman who works at the company was about her most recent racialized experience on the job. A white coworker placed a cotton plant on her desk and told her to pick it. I'm sure you can imagine how appalled the woman was. The man who did this was confronted about his distasteful act—he explained that he was simply joking.

Having spoken to the woman, it was evident to me that she didn't find the joke humorous. What was most disturbing to the black woman, as she stated it, was that this man felt comfortable with this kind of joking as an acceptable prank in his work environment. After more than ten years with the company, this woman had hoped that her dot of racial distinction was vanishing.

WHITE MALES

While these kinds of racial tensions and offenses still exist, minorities aren't the only ones feeling misjudged and prejudged. White males are beginning to get frustrated with what inclusion might mean for them in this increasingly multicultural society.

In the case of the dotted interview experiment, imagine the white male as the interviewer. After the interview one of the interviewees states, "He was staring at my dot the whole time"—he is a dotist, in other words. The interviewee didn't realize that there was no dot on her face. How do you think the interviewer feels as he honestly protests that his interaction with the interviewee was not influenced by the presence or absence of a dot? Both persons feel hurt and misunderstood.

America finds itself at a time in history when the white male is becoming a minority figure. For the past number of centuries this majority-ruled country has been under the rule of the white majority. The white man, as he sees the world around him becoming more and more multicultural, realizes that in the times when he used to feel "in," now he feels "out," and it's hard to come to terms with how someone can feel "out" in their own country. The white man has a dot of his own. Some whites may already feel as if they are prejudged and labeled as racists. They may have heard people use phrases like white supremacy, white privilege, or white dominance, and feel condemned before they even have a chance to speak. It feels unconscionable to be told that just because you are white, your opinions on issues of social justice are invalid and you are now excluded from the table of diversity. Whites are beginning to feel accused and victimized by public opinion and labeled as the oppressor. There was a time when the majority of white men enjoyed their positions of power as a privilege that was unchallenged. Now the push for diversity and multiculturalism feels threatening, and many white men are wondering whether they are a part of the inclusion.

Many of my white male brothers do not want to be associated with racism, injustice, or abusive power. They are tired of being prejudged before they are even given a chance to speak. God forbid that they slip and use the wrong terminology as it relates to other races or gender. These men are feeling the squeeze. Some are fully engaged in the cultural shift and welcome the opportunity to include others, while other white men remain resentful and protective of positions of power and privilege. If diversity is done right, everyone—including whites—should feel welcomed at the table of ideas and influence.

I have many white friends who hold a position of trust in my life. They have never launched racial epithets at minorities, they worship at multicultural churches, they don't say "all lives matter," and they don't refer to people of color as "thugs" or "those people." Yet they, and even some of my Asian and Latino friends, have been accused of racism simply for having lighter skin. They have been told that the only access to the conversation is through the door of guilt and shame. I believe strongly, however, that although my white brothers should reflect on how they might be contributing to racial hurt and systems of injustice, self-loathing should not be a prerequisite for inclusion in the journey toward racial healing. What do you think, is this dotism or disagreement?

REVERSE WHITES VERSUS DIVERSE WHITES

What I have learned over the years about some white folks is that the changing demographics in North America are unsettling to them as the population is becoming more brown. Some call it the browning of America. Many of our white brothers and sisters feel like their status of power and control is being threatened by multiculturalism.

Those who I call "reverse" whites have a deep longing to make America what it was before. They desire and even openly fight for an America that is less diverse and more safe. The "more safe" feeling doesn't include black people, brown people, immigrants, women, and the LGBTQ+ community. Safety was, and is, defined by a world where whites do not need to make any adjustments to their social order. It is a world where everyone who is different from them must adjust to their world of privilege, prominence, and power. They contend with the feeling of being replaced by others and are deeply offended by ideas where they cannot control the narrative. In fact, they are deeply offended by having to make any adjustments.

I talked to one white woman who was absolutely irate because she had to "press 1" for English at the ATM when she wanted to access a banking service. I was amazed by how offended she was because she was so inconvenienced to be required to push an extra button one time. The mere fact of having to be minimally inclusive of people who spoke Spanish was enough to send her over the edge emotionally. For this white woman, it was as if whites were being persecuted and were now suffering at the hands of multiculturalism. This was unbelievable to me!

Reverse whites want to protect their status of systematic advantage and will rigorously do whatever it takes to turn the clock back to a time in history that was best for their period of dominance.

Diverse whites, on the other hand, realize that they are a part of a greater mosaic of people and are called on to live in a world where everyone has equality, opportunity, and dignity. They recognize that their status is based on their humanity, and not on the social construct of superiority of whiteness or inferiority of nonwhiteness.

As a result, diverse whites learn how to adjust, shift, understand, and empathize with others with whom they share the planet. Instead of resenting pressing 1 for English, they recognize that although English is the majority language of North America, our society is inclusive and many languages are spoken. Diverse whites realize that all dots are not created equal and that some people may have more dots than others. They are aware that sometimes people may wrongly accuse them of dotism or racism because of their history and the negative experiences that people of color have endured to this day. Instead of denying and dismissing the negative experiences of people of color, diverse whites seek to understand and empathize with those who have not enjoyed the in-group majority status of dominance since the beginning of the nation's founding.

I am happy to say that I know, worship with, and have many family members who are diverse whites. I believe that if our nation, churches, campuses, and organizations are going to advance in the work of reconciliation, then we will need more and more diverse whites in our country. We will also need diverse whites to build bridges with reverse whites in ways that people of color may not have access, credibility, or opportunity to.

A SIN PROBLEM

Racism is not reserved for one color or culture of people. The sin of racism is an equal opportunity employer. (Or should I say, an equal opportunity destroyer?) Racism is not simply a skin problem but is a sin problem. While this may sound like a cliché, we must continue to sound the alarm that God hates this sin because he so loves this world. Continual reminders of the spiritual impact that sin has on people, including the sin of racism, are important so that everyone can see the negative consequences that affect many. All have sinned; all can sin, regardless of race. Therefore, it is important to note that blacks and other minorities can be racists too.

While walking down the street one day, I heard a black man using racially pejorative language referring to Mexicans. It made me think about the universality of sin, regardless of race. Even in my own multicultural church we have to disciple people out of racist mindsets. We have heard and confronted negative racial language about Asians, whites, blacks, Arabs, and Hispanics. This transforming of our mind must reach into how we view those that come across our southern border, those we go to serve on mission trips, and those refugees that have moved into our neighborhood. Wherever there is ethnic difference combined with a societal power imbalance, you have the potential for the destructive sin of racism.

All people struggle with sins rooted in the history of superiority, inferiority, and greed. This includes not only Europeans, Spaniards, and white Americans who perpetrated slavery and colonialism, but also some Africans who sold their brothers and sisters into American slavery hundreds of years ago. It further includes the many aware countries, corporations, and religious denominations that either turned their heads or directly benefited from the horrors of American slavery.

NOT ALL DOTS ARE EQUAL

Does the phrase "Sneetches on Beaches" ring a bell to you? If it does, then you probably remember the Dr. Seuss book in which the fictional characters called Sneetches invent new ways to apply or remove stars from their bellies in order to either gain acceptance to the in-group or to become more exclusive to keep others out. This never-ending cycle of comparison was fueled by one thing—the in-group had the societal power to exclude. The in-group had the leverage to declare what was normal, who was invited, and what qualities were valuable. The in-group was in control.

It might be tempting, as we begin to acknowledge the many layers of racial division, damage, and disparity, to begin to view all discrimination or prejudice equally. However, I want to caution you to not lose sight of how important it is to always ask the question, "Who has the societal power to exclude?" In our majority-ruled country, the power that a person has by simply being part of a majority group often goes unnoticed by the one who is in that in-group. Dotism might reveal the commonality of exclusion that we all face regardless of color, class, and culture, but racism emerges when we realize that not all dots are equal. The challenges of cultural tension that white majority folks face must not be seen as equivalent to the impact of the historical abuses, near genocide of people groups, and weight of assimilation that ethnic minorities are wrestling with and still attempting to recover from. The complex systems surrounding, supporting, and sustaining racism against people of color are unique among discriminatory divisions. The widespread and deep-rooted racial injustices that have plagued our country require us to move with focused compassion and commitment to heal their deep wounds. Although we are all a part of this healing process, I implore my white brothers and sisters to resist the urge to rush to say, "What about me? I'm discriminated against too," but instead start with, "If this is important to you, I will make it important to me."

EVERYONE HAS A DOT

We now live in a country that is standing face-to-face with the challenges of pulling itself out of the muddy waters of racism as an acceptable public practice. While for some this is a journey you have been on for a long time, for others you are just beginning to walk this path. Identifying our shared hardship of dotism helps us to begin to see the very personal presence of discrimination in our world. We know that in North America everyone has some sort of dot of distinction. Whether white, black, Mexican, female, male, gay, straight, disabled, or overweight, we can find much commonality in our experience of feeling the division that comes from dotism.

Everyone has the capability of putting someone else down based on that person's color, culture, class, or other distinction. No matter its form, dotism still exists because sin still exists. And would it not be a tragedy to see people of color turn around and become the most vicious dotists of all against others? Would it not be a terrible cultural shift to see women step on the masculinity of their gender counterparts to gain their liberation? Whether the pendulum of dotism swings to one extreme or the other, it is just as debased and evil. Addressing this dotism can be our shared pathway forward in addressing the deeper, more complex issues of racism that have overwhelmed so many for so long.

There must be an answer to dotism that doesn't leave people feeling left out, judged, and discriminated against. There must be an answer for those in the power position who want to face the harsh realities of our past without being forced into self-loathing and guilt. There must be a theological response to racism in the culture and racial segregation in the church. Right? There is—it's gracism.

2

FROM RACISM
TO GRACISM

I define *racism* as speaking, acting, or thinking negatively about someone else solely based on that person's color, class, or culture. A common definition for *grace* is the unmerited favor of God on humankind. Extending such favor and kindness on other human beings is how we Christians demonstrate this grace practically from day to day. When one merges the definition of racism, which is negative, with the definition of grace, which is positive, a new term emerges—*gracism*. I define *gracism* as the positive extension of favor to others regardless of and sometimes because of their color, class, or culture.

FAVOR OR FAVORITISM?

The extension of favor has biblical merit. The apostle Paul encouraged the Galatians, "As we have opportunity, let us do good to all people, especially to those who belong to the family of believers" (Galatians 6:10).

The positive extension of favor toward certain people does not have to mean favoritism. When James wrote about favoritism, he was writing in the context of loving all people and not discriminating against those who are underresourced, low-class or poor. "If you really keep the royal law found in Scripture, 'Love your neighbor as yourself,' you are doing right. But if you show favoritism, you sin and are convicted by the law as lawbreakers" (James 2:8-9).

To discriminate, exclude, and not love everyone is sin. Notice that James's comments about favoritism in verse 9 follow the command to love your neighbor in verse 8. His point is that we are to love everyone and not discriminate against anyone. Does this mean that extending positive favor in an environment where everyone is loved and treated with equal respect is wrong? I say no. Even God is shown to give extra attention to the poor, the needy, the orphans, and widows throughout the whole of Scripture. Consider how God made the effort to visit Hagar in a special way even though she was a single mom who should not have been impregnated by Abram.

Hagar was a victim of Abram and Sarai's lack of faith, because they didn't believe God's promise that they would have a child. Sarai suggested that Abram sleep with Hagar as a surrogate mother to produce a child; Hagar had little say in the matter. Later, as a single mother who was impregnated by Abram, mistreated by Sarai, and then cast aside as someone who was simply a baby incubator, Hagar fled into the desert to escape her intolerable situation (Genesis 16:6-7).

Notice how God proactively reached out to Hagar: "The angel of the LORD found Hagar near a spring in the desert; it was the spring that is beside the road to Shur. And he said, 'Hagar, servant of Sarai, where have you come from, and where are you going?'" (Genesis 16:7-8).

After the conversation with the angel of the Lord, Hagar "gave this name to the LORD who spoke to her: 'You are the God who sees me,' for she said, 'I have now seen the One who sees me'" (Genesis 16:13). After this Hagar gave birth to a son named Ishmael, which means "hears." Hagar named God "the one who sees," and she had a child who she was instructed to name "hears."

God hears and sees those who are marginalized and misused. Even when others don't notice you, God notices you. When others don't see you, God sees you. In those moments when it feels like no one is listening to you, God hears you and is paying attention. This is the heart of a gracist; the one who hears, sees, and pays attention to those on the margins—those in the desert—is a gracist. God shows us through his actions with Hagar what the heart and art of inclusion look like.

With this new confidence, Hagar was able to return to the household from which she came because she had been graced by God. God went out of his way to minister to Hagar, an Egyptian woman who wasn't an heir to the Abrahamic promise. The Lord knew that Hagar had been a victim and was without covering, so he intentionally pursued her, listened to her, paid attention to her, and communicated with her. Such understanding was all Hagar needed in order to survive in the dysfunctional home she came from. As a divine gracist, God included Hagar in his network of care by ministering to her directly from heaven.

IS GRACISM FAIR?

Is it possible to extend favor and still be fair? Distinct from favoritism, whereby one is granted favor because of a special status, ethnic superiority, or commonality, gracism reaches outside the box of elitism and special favors based on some fraternal code or secret handshake. *Favor* is showering extra grace on a few while having love for all. *Favoritism* is purposefully neglecting the needs of the many to accommodate the greed of a few. While favor is the art of inclusion, favoritism is the exercise of exclusion. Christianity is an inclusive faith that bids all to come.

Yes, it is possible to extend favor without engaging in favoritism. There is a profound difference. One is from God and the other is from human beings.

WATER IN THE PIPES

Gracism even helps to reverse the patterns and practices of destructive favoritism that we have unknowingly become accustomed to. If we are always expecting racism to be overt, consciously deliberate, and hatefully committed by aggressive individuals, we are in danger of missing its pervasiveness in our society. We know that gracism addresses how racism shows up in our individual thoughts, speech, and actions, but gracism also gives us the opportunity to look at how we can combat the wider societal barriers people can face because of their race. In order to stop the flow of racism completely, we have to cut the flow off at the source and address the water still left in the pipes.

For example, when I was planning on going away on vacation for the first time after becoming a homeowner, someone reminded me to make sure I turned off the water to prevent any major flooding in my house, just in case something happened with my plumbing while I was away. After they told me where to find the valve to shut off the flow of water into the house, they informed me of an extra step to take before I was finished. They told me to open up all the faucets in the house to drain out the water that was still left in the pipes. They even went so far as to remind me to make sure I opened the faucets in the basement, so as to ensure I emptied out any residual pockets of water. It's a good thing, because I was shocked when the water kept flowing from the faucet even after I had cut off the source of the flow and emptied what was left from the other levels. With the water turned off at the source and all of the pipes drained, I could rest assured that I had safeguarded my home.

As we look to rid this world of racism, this plumbing analogy can help us understand that sometimes racial inequality and abuse is not just perpetuated by individuals but can be found in the patterns of operating that many institutions officially have on the books or unofficially repeat in practices that are just considered normal. When people talk about combating structural or systemic racism, I think of it like that plumbing system. Cutting off the water at the source is similar to an organizational leader instituting new official policy that halts practices that show favoritism to those in the majority culture and seeks to operate in a more equitable way. However, we cannot forget that there is water still left in the pipes. Just because the leader has put ink to paper to make the right changes, every community, organization, and church has un-official practices that have never been written down, are hard to define, and are near invisible. These habitual ways of doing things can continue to unknowingly show favoritism to some while excluding, repressing, or oppressing others.

This realization is particularly important for those of us who are in positions of influence or leadership; we have the power to set new norms and make decisions that can increase the reach of these gracism principles throughout our organizations, corporations, families, and schools. There is a danger that arises for folks who make progress in relationships with people who are different from themselves and then begin to think friendship is enough—that if more and more people would be nicer to people of a different race, we wouldn't have these problems in the world. We can ignore the fact that in many institutions, the destructive flow of favoritism has not been cut off at the source, and there is still residual accumulation left in the network of pipes. We can dismiss deeply ingrained patterns of living that were built over decades and longer, which were engineered with the success of only a certain people group in mind.

Systemic gracism emerges when a person of influence takes these gracism principles of strategically extending favor and applies them to transform the official policy and unofficial practices of the communities they lead, in order to cultivate an environment where everyone flourishes together.

A GRACIST LESSON LEARNED

I have been teaching on gracism for almost twenty years now. Although some people are early adopters, I often see that the teaching takes a while to take root. It is a slow and dawning truth that becomes clearer the more one has the opportunity to act on it. One woman who has been listening and learning about the concept of gracism wrote me an encouraging email to explain how the teaching had a surprising effect on her during an encounter she had while awaiting a flight in an airport queue.

> Last year I was in line at the airport waiting to board my flight on Southwest Airlines. I love Southwest for their cheap fares, but the one thing I don't like is that they have no assigned seats. You can print out your boarding group pass that will have an A, B, or C on it and then you wait in line till your group is called. Everyone wants a good seat on the plane, so people will stand in that line for an hour if they have to, myself included.

I was holding tightly to my boarding group pass, which said "A," and I had been waiting in that line for at least a half hour, when a family—husband, wife, and two young children—loudly made their way into the "waiting to board" area. You couldn't help but notice them. They seemed confused and were talking loudly in Spanish to one another, glancing at their tickets, waving their arms, and pulling their bags and their kids into the huddle of travelers. I thought perhaps they were Mexican, and I began trying to understand what they were saying, but my very limited Spanish failed me.

It's funny how these boarding group lines may not look like lines at all in the literal sense. They snake around tables, chairs, and luggage; they dip with younger travelers sitting down in the middle; they have big gaps where someone has stopped to talk on his cell phone or finish a page in her novel. But just to be clear—they are indeed lines. And it is understood who is in front of you and who is in back of you, and your place in the line is respected by the other travelers. Usually. The loud Spanish-speaking family was trying to work their way into the A line and ended up just a few people ahead of me, looking very confused. They were hanging just to the right of the line and you could tell they were hoping to somehow get absorbed into a real spot. The others in line were not happy about this. I watched the people get closer to one another and even position the men with them to stand on the side like a defensive line on a football team.

This family kept trying to get in, all the while looking confused, glancing at their tickets, and speaking in Spanish. They tried to slip in a few different places, but this line was a united front—no one was moving. All eyes were on them, and though no one said a word, the sound was deafening. I could see them shaking their heads in disgust. I could only imagine what was going through the minds of those in line. *Stupid foreigners. Who do they think they are coming over here and just butting in? They have no sense.* It didn't matter that no one was speaking this stuff out loud. I had heard it so many times and I could see it on their faces and in their body language. And part of me was feeling it too. *I have waited in this line all this time; no way are these people gonna just butt in front of me. That's not fair! Don't they know the rules? We just don't do that here. This is my place in line.*

Just as I was perfecting my speech in my head, full of righteous indignation and knowing full well that I was—we all were—right, I had a Holy Spirit smackdown. That's when a completely different thought comes into your brain that you know is of God and it feels like a smack upside your head. I don't like Holy Spirit smackdowns. This time it was your voice, David, in my head, talking about gracism. Special favor for those who are disregarded. Special treatment, going above and beyond to extend grace to those who have been oppressed and dismissed in this world because of their race, class, or culture.

It was such a powerful teaching and God used it to smack me upside the head in that moment. I prayed silently and asked God to help me be a gracist. He immediately showed me that my judgment of these people was wrong. Did it really matter who was in front of me in line? Who cares! What was most important here? What if you were in another country where you didn't speak the language and you were confused, tired, and fearing you weren't going to make it on the plane? How would you feel? Wouldn't you be looking for someone to show you some kindness?

So I stuck my head out of line just enough to tap the Mexican woman on the shoulder. "Excuse me. Please come over here. You can get in line right here in front of me." I knew she didn't understand my words, but my message came through loud and clear. She smiled at me so big I thought she was going to cry. She grabbed her husband and kids and they all kept thanking me and bowing their heads. I saw relief come to them as they took their spot in line in front of me. They were so grateful and I was so ashamed. Why had it taken me so long to do the right thing?

David, thank you for teaching me about gracism. While I never thought I was a racist, I see how even being silent in those moments feeds the problem. Considering others who are different and giving them special favor is unnatural for most people, but it's clearly in the Word of God, and now that I have had the chance to apply it, I can say it feels like God too.

SAYING "ALL LIVES MATTER"

When you show favor to some it might sometimes feel like you are not including all. We saw this come to center focus with the rise of the phrase *Black Lives Matter*. Many majority folks in our society did not know how to intellectually process the idea of extending extra favor to the black community during this period of time through the use of this phrase. Instead of focusing on the community in pain and reassuring them of the value of their lives, the focus was put on the organization Black Lives Matter, and we saw a new phrase come alive: *All Lives Matter.*

Imagine with me: You wake up in the middle of the night and make your way to the bathroom. As you stumble through the dark half asleep, you accidentally jam your big toe against the corner of your bed. With a scream of pain, you feel the shock of agony throughout your entire body, and within an instant a sound comes out of your mouth: "Ouch!" Maybe you use other choice words in the moment.

While that one big toe is writhing with pain, how ridiculous would it be for your other nine toes to begin protesting, "Hey, all toes matter! We other nine toes are important too, aren't we?"

When my brothers and sisters from the black community say "Black Lives Matter," they are emphasizing the pain of their collective "ouches" that cause them to writhe with emotional, mental, and often physical pain that comes from the realities of being black in America.

The big toe needs attention in the moment, not to the exclusion of the other toes. As the blood in the body rushes to the place of greatest pain, the rest of the body must accommodate and redirect its attention to bring triage and healing to the part of the body that needs the greatest healing in the moment.

Yes, all lives matter. All toes matter. Understanding the cries of pain when certain parts of the body are damaged is not dismissing the value of the other parts of the body. Rushing to value the part of the body that hurts is a natural response when trying to heal what is broken.

African Americans in our country for generations have suffered broken toes that have come not simply because of accidental stubbing but because of many systemic and institutional forces that have intentionally stepped on, and even crushed, the toes of the black community. When we say "Black Lives Matter," we are saying that it is high time to stop crushing the toes of black people. In fact, let's give attention to healing that which has been injured and damaged so that all the toes on the foot can enjoy walking without constant pain. This is an act of favor. This is an act of gracism.

GOD IN FRONT

When one puts a G, which stands for God, in front of the negative concept of racism, then one has begun identifying solutions and resources to address the race problem in the world. It may sound simplistic, but I believe it is right. Who said that the solution had to be difficult? Admittedly, the implementation of the solution is the most difficult. Why is this? Race problems bring with them anger, bitterness, prejudice, and pride. Conversion brings with it forgiveness, patience, and access to available resources, such as the filling and the fruit of the Spirit.

When we repent of our sins personally, corporately, and nationally, then we can begin to rebuild on a new foundation. Radical conversion and forgiveness change the heart of a person. Therefore, unless we go through repentance over the sin of racism, we Christians are battling the problem of race just like the world—namely without God. But if Christians put God in front of any problem, that problem will diminish because God is bigger than it. I am not saying that it will keep me as a black man from getting stopped by police officers when I'm traveling in neighborhoods that make them suspicious of me, but the God in me can give me the grace to handle such incidents that often produce legitimate fear in people that look like me, with patience, kindness, a measured response, and forgiveness.

A gracist reaches across ethnic lines and racial borders to lend assistance and "extra grace" to those who are different, on the fringe, or marginalized. This person or group can be of any color, culture, or gender.

Are you a gracist? The heart of a gracist extends a helping hand to those who are outside the positive norms of a particular society. While the majority may enjoy the hidden rules of a particular sociological group, gracists build bridges of inclusion for those on the margins. Just as God reached out to Hagar to comfort her in the desert of life, so we can minister to those who are desperate for someone to hear them and see them.

3

THE ART OF
INCLUSION

Inclusion makes sense purely for sociological reasons based on the demographics that are facing the United States. Did you know that almost 50 percent of the American population is expected to be made up of racial and ethnic minorities by 2045? The 2020 census data confirmed that non-Hispanic whites dropped in population majority from 76 percent in 1990 to 57.8 percent. Four out of ten people in America are members of minority groups, while 33.8 million people identified themselves as multiracial on the 2020 census, which is up from 6.8 million in the 2000 census. That's a 500 percent increase.

While the percentages I mention are just numbers on a page, they are represented by José, Juan, Shaquita, and Lequisha in the Walmart and Target stores within twenty minutes of most people's homes. Immigration has made the Hispanic population the largest minority group, while blacks come in at 46.9 million, and Asians and Pacific Islanders (AAPI) have grown to 20.7 million and continue to be the fastest-growing minority group. The AAPI community also holds the title of having the highest levels of ancestral diversity. School populations reflect the increased minority populations to such a degree that cultural proficiency programs are becoming a must. The school system that my racially mixed kids attended not only is diverse but also is becoming more competent in furthering the dialogue needed to ensure a safe and harmonious educational experience. Black immigrants from the Caribbean and Africa now number over four million and more than tripled since 2000. At the current rate, the United States will have no single majority racial or ethnic group by the middle of the twenty-first century.

In the year 2022 my church, Bridgeway, launched the very first Gracism Academy for Young Leaders. The call went out for emerging leaders between the ages of eighteen and twenty-nine to apply to join a cohort of other like-minded peers to spend six months learning how to integrate the principles of gracism into their rising careers and relationships. When I came to speak at the first gathering and laid eyes on the group that was selected for this initiative, it was like looking into our future. This group of thirteen was made up of people with heritage from around the world. As a part of this one cohort we had people who were African American, Filipino/Korean, American-born Nigerian, black/white, Filipino American, Korean/black, Puerto Rican/black, white, and Slovak/Ethiopian. In addition, one of the leaders is Gujarati Indian and the other is white. And they serve under the covering of this black pastor. Wow, this is not just our future but it is our reality today!

Including people from various backgrounds in our lives and ministries not only is savvy sociologically but also is biblical. The Bible makes it clear that the Lord desires to reach people from every nation. I also believe that we need each other in order for the body to work together as God has designed his church to do and be.

A NEW VIEW

Many have come across 1 Corinthians 12 in sermons, Bible studies, or casual reading of the Bible when studying the spiritual gifts or musing on biblical unity. When I was reading devotionally through the passage one time, questions related to verses 12 and 13 began to surface in my mind. I wondered why Paul, the author of this text, would include such "irrelevant" verses. I raised an eyebrow and thought that the verses didn't belong in the text at all.

In verse 12 Paul gives an analogy of the human body to illustrate his earlier point about differences regarding spiritual manifestations. He writes, "Just as a body, though one, has many parts, but all its many parts form one body, so it is with Christ" (1 Corinthians 12:12). But then, before unpacking and expanding on this analogy, Paul interjects race and culture. How forced, it seemed to me. How unpoetic. How off topic. But the truth is, the apostle purposefully put into place something important that he did not want us to miss. I had indeed missed it until now. "For we were all baptized by one Spirit so as to form one body—whether Jews or Gentiles, slave or free—and we were all given the one Spirit to drink" (1 Corinthians 12:13).

Whoa! Did you notice what Paul did here? He mentioned race and culture (Jews or Greeks) and class (slave or free). He did more than simply insert an abstract thought about race and culture. The author was making a transition. He was telling us how we are to view the rest of the passage.

Paul wanted us to read verse 14 and the following through the lenses of race, culture, and class. To avoid reading the rest of the passage in that way would do violence to the writer's intent. Thus I appeal to you to read the next section slowly with these lenses on. Read it as if those whom you know with dots on their faces were sitting next to you. Keep race, culture, and class in mind as you read.

Even so the body is not made up of one part but of many.

Now if the foot should say, "Because I am not a hand, I do not belong to the body," it would not for that reason stop being part of the body. And if the ear should say, "Because I am not an eye, I do not belong to the body," it would not for that reason stop being part of the body. If the whole body were an eye, where would the sense of hearing be? If the whole body were an ear, where would the sense of smell be? But in fact God has placed the parts in the body, every one of them, just as he wanted them to be. If they were all one part, where would the body be? As it is, there are many parts, but one body.

The eye cannot say to the hand, "I don't need you!" And the head cannot say to the feet, "I don't need you!" On the contrary, those parts of the body that seem to be weaker are indispensable, and the parts that we think are less honorable we treat with special honor. And the parts that are unpresentable are treated with special modesty, while our presentable parts need no special treatment. But God has put the body together, giving greater honor to the parts that lacked it, so that there should be no division in the body, but that its parts should have equal concern for each other. If one part suffers, every part suffers with it; if one part is honored, every part rejoices with it.

Now you are the body of Christ, and each one of you is a part of it. (1 Corinthians 12:14-27)

Well, what do you think? Powerful, isn't it? When we read the above text through the lenses of race, culture, and class, it begins to have a clearer meaning. For me it had an entirely new meaning. I was floored when I read it afresh. I now have a new view of the passage. It has multiplied my understanding beyond the single view of addressing the diversity of spiritual gifts, to affirming the multiplicity of racial, ethnic, and class interdependency as well.

The writer is suggesting that we view all those in the body—those with dots, if you will—in a specific way. Anyone who may feel, look, or truly be "unpresentable" or "weaker" must be handled, and even honored, differently. No one should be on the fringes without others reaching out to include them, whether white or black, Jewish or Arab, Hmong or Laotian, rich or poor, male or female.

Allow me to take creative license in paraphrasing the text using my own words and imagination. (Maybe you'd like to do the same to help you make the passage a practical reality in your friendships, fellowships, and family.)

> Now the body is not made up of one culture but of many. If the blacks should say to the whites, "Because I am not white, I do not belong to the body," it would not make it true. The blacks would still be a part of the body whether they vote for the same candidates or not. And if the whites should say, "Because I am not black, I do not belong to the body," it would not make it true. The whites would still be a part of the body whether they clapped their hands and shouted loudly in church or not. It doesn't mean that they are not filled with the Spirit. If the whole body was tightly structured, where would the sense of spontaneity be? If the whole body was sponta-neous, where would the sense of order be? As it is, there are many parts and many cultures, but one body.
>
> The Cuban church cannot say to the Haitian church, "I don't need you!" The Puerto Rican church cannot say

to the Mexican church, "I don't need you!" The Pakistanis cannot say to the Persians, "I don't need you!" The Japanese cannot say to the Koreans, "I don't need you!" The suburban church cannot say to the urban church, "I don't need you!" The city church cannot say to the country church, "I don't need you!" Jews cannot say to Arabs, "I don't need you!" Palestinians cannot say to Jews, "I don't need you!" On the contrary, those parts of the body that seem to be weaker are not to be dismissed or discarded as if they don't matter. They are God's special instruments of honor to reveal an aspect of God that would otherwise not be seen or experienced. There really is no part of the Christian body that is to be dismissed as unimportant. They all matter! If Palestinian Christians suffer, we all suffer. If South African Christians are freed from apartheid, we all rejoice with them. Now you are the body of Christ, and each one of you is a part of it.

PRACTICAL CHURCH GRACISM

At Bridgeway Community Church, where I pastor, we have canceled service elements, rearranged stage designs, accommodated staff positions, and even added new team members with an eye to color and culture. Yes, you can call me a gracist and I won't be mad if you do! I hope I'm guilty as charged.

A gracist recognizes the beauty of diversity. A gracist will go to any length and work as diligently as possible to ensure that such beauty is seen and celebrated. A gracist truly believes that everyone brings value, has worth, and should be included. Gracists refuse to settle for unicultural segregation without doing all they can to include diversity at all levels of the church. This includes those in leadership and those in the

pew. A gracist can't help but think about those in the neighborhood who are of a different color than the congregants.

Imagine a local pastor asking himself or herself the following
questions about the people in the target ministry area from
different colors, cultures, and classes: *What's wrong? Why don't
they come in? What can I do to build a bridge? What is my
church communicating that is keeping them away? What is
my church missing by not having these people as a part of our
fellowship?* These are the persistent questions of a gracist. They
are good questions to ask and even tougher to answer but are
important to invest brainpower and prayer power in.

Think about your church. Think about your small group or
Bible class. Think about the people in your family and in your
household on a daily, weekly, or monthly basis. Are they all
from the same color, culture, or class? Now think about Christ.
If he were to have a dinner party, a small Bible study group, a
church service, or a family meeting, do you think everyone
would be from the same color, culture, or class? Don't we all
want to be more like Christ? I am forced to ask myself, *Am I
reflecting the life of Christ as a gracist or reflecting the life of a
racist? Am I perpetuating segregation among Christians and
simply justifying it with my preferences and comfort? Am I a
bridge builder of reconciliation?* Maybe your life is lived somewhere between the two extremes. You aren't a racist and yet
you've not become a gracist either. For instance, maybe you
have the heart of Christ to be more inclusive but are not in a
location, church, or environment that allows you to regularly
interact with people from a different racial, ethnic, or socio-
economic background. So what are you to do?

I suggest that every person living in a unicultural environment prepare their heart to be a reconciler in every area
because the principles of God's Word, when it comes to

reconciliation, work in all arenas. This includes the principle of gracism.

There are people on the fringe in your church who may be the same color as the majority of your church members but who are still in need of inclusion. There are people in your family, on your job, in your community, who are in need of gracist inclusion. As you embrace and develop your calling to be a gracist, God will give you more opportunities than you can imagine to live it out. When you exercise the muscles of gracism with the marginal people you already know, your muscles will be strengthened and prepared to handle more gracist opportunities.

MONUMENTAL

After the murder of George Floyd, a black man killed at the hands of a white Minneapolis police officer in the spring of 2020, many church leaders who had been courting the idea of speaking to the racial tension that our country had been experiencing sensed that they could no longer stay quiet in the conversation. Many of them had watched the traumatizing video and, in spite of the usual arguments that typically blame the victim for contributing to their own death, they could not un-see what came to be described as a modern-day public lynching. Although there had been previous instances of black men losing their lives at the hands of police, this one sparked something monumental. Maybe it was because of the video footage, maybe it was because of the other recent news stories of racist abuse and murder, or maybe it was because of the increased isolation and alienation the people of this country had been experiencing.

For whatever reason, pastors around the country felt it was time to engage. Sermons were given, statements were released, and many ministry leaders from around the country reached out to me for advice. One African American pastor in New Jersey got in touch with me for guidance after the pastor of a local white church in his community wanted to do a pulpit swap and host joint discussion events.

The energy around multicultural ministry and racial justice in the church had never been this widely engaged; some churches were more prepared than others, some churches did it better than others, some congregations received the messages more readily than others. Some white pastors spoke too quickly without first taking time to listen and some Asian pastors questioned where their voice was welcomed into the conversation, while some of my African American brothers and sisters were so overcome with grief that they couldn't even speak at all.

One thing was clear after all of the activity that year—to see the church address the division, damage, and disparity caused by racism, to make real change in this area, we would need a plan, we would need each other, we would need action, we would need patience, and we would need Jesus.

Many churches that spoke up quickly in 2020 have gone back to their typical sermon series, and you would be hard-pressed to find evidence of their brief engagement in this issue. Other churches have maintained a commitment to build bridges across racial lines and are doing the necessary work to transform the inclusivity of their communities. I often walk alongside pastors and marketplace leaders who are making strides in creating an environment where those who have been hurt, those who have done the hurting, those who are hesitant, and those who are just waking up to the importance of these issues can use the principles found in the 1 Corinthians verses to build gracist cultures that walk this rocky road of racial healing. I wonder how you would describe your journey of engagement on these monumental issues.

DAVID THE MENACE?

I still remember how hard is was for me to shake the feelings of being a sellout when I received a nasty letter—hate mail— one day when I arrived at my office desk. The letter was riddled with words of anger, poisonous verbiage, and accusation. The letter was evidently from an angry African American man who thought that my preaching, teaching, and radio hosting about multiculturalism offered a dangerous and potentially harmful message for and against the black church. He called me a "menace" to the black church.

I could not disagree more. I've never read a text of Scripture that outlines God's design for a one-race church. I grew up in the black church, and I love the history and upbringing that it afforded me. My dad was a pastor and church planter all my life. I respect the tradition of my family and the heritage it represents. Having said this, I don't believe that the Scriptures mandate a fierce protection of racial and denominational institutions. As much as I love the black church and at times miss it, there will be no black church in heaven. There will be one church and it will be multicultural. One bride, not a harem, is what Jesus is coming back for.

Do I see a role for the black church? Of course I do. Just as I see a role for ethnic churches that are catch basins for foreign-born immigrants. But this does not mean that unicultural churches that have a unique function are the end-all of God's vision for his church. Such unicultural churches should still be moving toward multiculturalism in some way to prepare their members to love and reflect Christ to all people. This is the teaching of true discipleship, is it not? Did Jesus not command and commission his followers to make disciples of all nations? No church or Christian is exempt in playing a part in this magnanimous vision from on high. All churches—black, white, and others—must train their members to become the gracists that God desires all his ambassadors of reconciliation to be.

Just as I am an arrow shot from my family of origin into a multicultural world where I must contribute to society in an effective and godly way, so ethnic churches must see their role in preparing their members for greater multicultural influence and proficiency as Christian ambassadors. As a son of my parents and as a sibling, I can honor my parents and my family history without being constrained by my family's limitations. If my parents did a good job, then I should be a well-adjusted husband, father, and church leader.

I can say that I have learned to be gracious and gracist because of the lessons my mother taught about forgiveness when a white neighbor kid called me a "n-----" continually. I learned gentleness and negotiation from my dad after he spoke privately with two of my black friends when they refused to be my friend for a summer. Dad offered each of them one dollar and they became my friends again. How cheap I felt after I learned about this many months later! I thought I was worth at least five dollars as a friend. Yet these same friends became even closer buddies when we were chased through the neighborhood by white hippies, who hollered obscenities at us while circling the block again and again in their hot rod with the windows down, shooting BB pellets at us. We were eight years old and too scared to leave our hiding place in the neighborhood for hours. When Dad discovered what had happened he called the police, and he comforted us. I learned how to handle anger appropriately and not hysterically from my father.

I not only remember these stories from my upbringing, but also I honor and celebrate the kind of family I was raised in. But just because I was raised in a unicultural family doesn't mean that I am to stay in one. In fact I am thankful to have been prepared in my unicultural family to survive and succeed in a multicultural world. It is upon that foundation that I write about gracism. My parents adequately prepared me, not poisoned me, regarding race and grace. May this be true for every unicultural environment, families and churches in particular.

How does one prepare the soil? How do churches raise a generation of gracists? What can each of us do to be a gracist? The next several chapters address specific behaviors that can help us live out the principles of gracism in a practical way.

I have identified eight phrases from 1 Corinthians 12 as gracist sayings. We will look at a saying in each of the next eight chapters and give clear suggestions on how to integrate the sayings into daily action. The sayings are italicized in the text below:

Those parts of the body that seem to be weaker are indispensable, and the parts that we think are less honorable we treat with *special honor.* And the parts that are unpresentable are treated with *special modesty,* while our presentable parts need *no special treatment.* But God has put the body together, giving *greater honor* to the parts that lacked it, so that there should be *no division in the body,* but that its parts should have *equal concern* for each other. If one part suffers, every part *suffers with it;* if one part is honored, every part *rejoices with it.* (1 Corinthians 12:22-26, emphasis added)

EIGHT SAYINGS OF A GRACIST

1. "I WILL LIFT YOU UP." *Special honor* means lifting up the humble by assisting and elevating them toward success.

2. "I WILL COVER YOU." *Special modesty* means protecting the most vulnerable among us from embarrassment and harm.

3. "I WILL SHARE WITH YOU." No *special treatment* means opening up networks and resources to others who are systemically downtrodden, and refusing to offer special treatment that may hurt them.

4. "I WILL HONOR YOU." *Greater honor* means recognizing those who are the most humble heroes among us and affirming the dignity of those we would otherwise dismiss.

5. "I WILL STAND WITH YOU." No *division* means the majority committing to stand up for the minority and the stronger helping the weaker.

6. "I WILL CONSIDER YOU." *Equal concern* means putting special focus on the perspectives and needs of those who are often overlooked.

7. "I WILL CELEBRATE WITH YOU." *Rejoices with it* means when the humble, or less honorable, are helped, we are to rejoice with them.

8. "I WILL HEAL WITH YOU." *Suffers with it* means empathizing with the pain of another and walking empathetically with the injured party.

4

Saying One:
I WILL LIFT YOU UP

*Those parts of the body that seem to be weaker are
indispensable, and the parts that we think are
less honorable we treat with special honor.*

1 Corinthians 12:22-23 (Emphasis Added)

In 1 Corinthians 12:23, the apostle Paul refers to treating others with "special honor." This means saying to others, "I will lift you up." A gracist is committed to lifting up others who are on the fringes, in the minority, or in need of extra attention.

Paul is saying that the people who have less honor because, let's say, their gifts lack public pizzazz or their pedigree is less than glowing, are the ones who need special honor. Sometimes we have to work hard to discover and lift up those seemingly hard-to-notice people who don't shine like the stars around us.

In my pastoral ministry, many of the people I work alongside are extremely gifted and skilled in ways that are visible to our entire community. They are the easier people to recognize. It takes extra work for me to scope out the hidden heroes, those servants who are making a major difference for the kingdom of God and yet are often overlooked. Such people may include volunteers in our children's ministry, folks working in the parking lots, servants on our technical team, or someone at an office workstation who keeps the administrative details of business in order. In addition to people with behind-the-scenes roles, those that tend to be more introverted can often go overlooked as well. It's not uncommon for church congregations to put a lower emphasis on those who do not gravitate toward large social gatherings.

Such individuals might be judged as weaker or not as important because they are not as visible. While none of us would openly call them weaker or dispensable, the way we act toward them or neglect them is evidence of their near invisibility.

LIFT AS THEY CLIMB

Oftentimes those who would benefit from another person lifting them up do not need the help because they have some kind of intrinsic deficiency, but instead they experience an exhaustion—weariness that comes from the challenges of overcoming the extra barriers they face because of the difficulty of their position. When starting and maturing their entrepreneurial ventures, black women face marketplace challenges that require extra strength and tenacity for them to achieve success as compared to their racial and gender counterparts. As gracists, we can keep an eye out for those who might have a unique type of struggle they are working to overcome and leverage our resources to help lift as they climb.

I met Cindy before she started her business, when she called into my radio show seeking a word from the Lord. The Spirit interrupted both of us that day when he gave me a uniquely personal word for her before she could even ask her question. It turns out the loss of her mother and the lack of responsibility of her adult siblings to help shoulder the financial responsibilities associated with her mother's funeral had left unresolved anger that the Lord wanted to minister to that day.

Because the clock was ticking and the show was about to end, I asked Cindy to hold the line so that I could talk with her after the show. When the show was over I continued talking with Cindy off the air. In addition to praying with her about her family members, I shared with Cindy that earlier that morning a friend donated five hundred dollars for me to pass on to anyone who God was leading me to bless. I believed that Cindy was the person that was supposed to receive this generous gift from my prayer partner and friend. When I told Cindy that we were going to bless her with this money, she was overwhelmed and overjoyed.

A few weeks later Cindy called the show again with a spirit of great joy. It was almost as if I were talking with a different person. Cindy mentioned that the gift was a blessing and that she was inspired to follow her dream to open a Jamaican restaurant. This took me off-guard because we had never discussed her dream to own a restaurant. However, the conversation, prayer, and unexpected gift of gracist generosity lifted her out of the doldrums and put her back on the path of dreaming again. One year later, Cindy opened her restaurant in southern Maryland.

When I heard that her restaurant was up and running, my gracist mindset sprung to action again. Knowing that black women often do not receive the same support and resources that others do, I wanted to do whatever I could to help lift her and her business toward success. In order to support her, I asked if I could host my radio show from her restaurant, tell her story, and invite my listeners to join me. Her joy of being seen, supported, and lifted in a way that propelled her toward success was infectious. Cindy's spirits were lifted. Our spirits were lifted. The spirits of the community were lifted. And we were able to lift up this black female entrepreneur as she faced unique challenges to achieve her dreams.

The Scripture writer reminds us that no one is dispensable and no one who is experiencing an exhaustion-weariness should be left in isolation to burn out in weakness. None of our brothers or sisters in Christ should feel like they have to fight on their own to overcome the barriers keeping them from success. This is especially true when those barriers are set up against them simply because of their color, class, culture, or gender. This was exactly Paul's point. We are to lift others up.

BUCK AND BIG TONY

After thirty-three years as a state trooper for the state of Maryland, Officer Gerald Wagner (also known as Buck) accepted the invitation of his girlfriend to attend Bridgeway Community Church, the church I pastor in Columbia, Maryland.

Buck didn't know the Lord, nor did he want to visit Bridgeway. His girlfriend, however, made a deal with him. "If you visit Bridgeway and find one thing wrong that you don't like," she said, "then you never have to attend again and I'll stop hounding you."

Buck saw this as a great deal. He reveled in the fact that he had to identify only one thing that displeased him and he could resume his regular Sunday habits of working on his car and watching football. Little did Buck know what God had in store.

I don't remember the sermon I preached on that Sunday, but I do remember extending an invitation for anyone in the congregation who wanted to receive Jesus Christ, as I periodically do as the Lord leads. God had a plan for Buck on this particular Sunday. As I extended the gospel invitation for salvation, Buck felt his legs stand him straight up. "As if I were the only sinner in the room," Buck states, "I felt God calling me to repentance specifically and personally." What a beautiful day that was for Buck, for his girlfriend, and for me as I led the congregation in a prayer to place faith in Jesus Christ! This was the day Buck crossed over from spiritual death to spiritual life.

As a new Christian, Buck was excited and ready to do life God's way. Turning away from the behaviors of his state trooper days and the sins of his youth, Buck turned to the church to serve. He alerted the church office that he didn't have skills to sing, dance, act, or preach, but if the church needed someone to move chairs, run errands, carry things, or transport people, he would be more than happy to serve in this way. One day my executive assistant asked Buck to drive me to the airport so that a staff member would not have to do so. Shortly thereafter Buck offered to drive me anywhere. He explained that he had driven for many official people, including the governor of our state. Buck convinced me that serving through driving was in no way imposing on him but, conversely, he would be more than happy to transport me to my weekly radio show—which was fifty miles from my house—to airports, meetings, and events throughout the major cities near our church, such as Washington, DC, Baltimore, Philadelphia, and New York. What a godsend! Who knew?

Subsequently Buck began driving me in his personal vehicle to ministry events. That is, until another member of the congregation, a man known as Big Tony who owns a limo company, offered me his vehicles as his own personal

ministry. Can you believe that? This offer was totally unexpected and unrelated to the driver whom God had provided
for me just weeks prior. Big Tony required, however, that I use
his employed drivers due to insurance requirements, and he
asked that his gift of service be anonymous. I committed to
being discreet about his generosity, but I couldn't commit to
using only his drivers, since God had already provided me
with one who had decades of experience driving all kinds of
people. After sharing this with the limo company owner, he
agreed to allow his cars to be available for Buck's use in trans-
porting me since he was a retired state trooper. I was amazed
by God's grace.

At first I struggled with whether or not I, as a minister,
should even embrace this gift of service. After careful consideration, why would I deny what God had clearly offered me as
a blessing? I have fully embraced this gift with thanksgiving
while trying to be as modest as I can.

Blessed with a car and a driver through no finagling of my
own, I unwittingly discovered how much I am taking advantage of this ministry as a stewardship opportunity in my
life. While en route I prepare for appointments, receive
briefings of upcoming engagements, review material for the
radio show, and conduct meetings with people. Sometimes,
when I am alone except for Buck, I just pray, reflect, or day-
dream while looking out the window. What a crazy and un-
likely gift—one that I didn't even realize could be leveraged
for ministry and would never have solicited for myself!
That's just like God, isn't it? God lifted me up in a unique and
specific way.

You may not have a car and driver, but you do need someone
to lift you up in specific ways that meet your particular needs,
right? God is the master planner and knows just how to

configure his people in such a way as to meet your every need. Do you believe this?

PRAYER

One practical way we can lift each other up is through prayer. Interceding on behalf of others who are underappreciated, undervalued, on the fringes, or different is a great way to elevate your care and concern for them. In relating gracefully to someone you are reaching out to, simply ask this person regularly about how you can pray for him or her. The next time you speak with the person you are lifting up, ask how things are going regarding the prayers that were requested. This person will be blessed to know that someone is lifting them up in prayer. We all are blessed by the intercession of others, but for those on the margins it feels even more rewarding to know that someone in the majority culture or a power position cares enough to be concerned with such matters.

In addition, to take the prayers of gracism to a higher level, ask the person to whom you are reaching out to pray for you. This takes you out of the superior position and places you under the grace and spiritual support of someone else who may otherwise have perceived that you are not in need of them but are there only to reach out. The exchange of gifts and the mutuality of lifts give dignity to human relationships. When I lift you up, you are blessed. Likewise, when I allow you to lift me up, while it may be humbling for me, it is dignifying for you.

Remember when Jesus asked the woman at the well for a drink of water in John 4? Jesus started the exchange by asking for something he needed. How dignifying! This woman, who may have lost all self-respect and dignity, must have been amazed by the fact that she was being asked to meet a Jewish man's need at the community well. Everyone has something to offer. Unfortunately, when we are in the power position, it becomes increasingly difficult to allow ourselves to be served in a spiritual way. Yet Jesus allowed himself to be served by this Samaritan woman.

The apostle Peter had a hard time with this concept when it was time for another water lesson. This time it had to do with Jesus washing Peter's feet (John 13:1-10). Peter thought it humiliating to allow himself to be served by Jesus. Yet Jesus clearly communicated to Peter that this must be done, not because Jesus needed dignifying like the woman at the well, but because Peter needed humbling.

This works as a leadership principle as well. Many leaders might pursue a diversity, equity, and inclusion (DEI) program from a philanthropic or social outreach perspective alone and miss a valuable layer to this new inclusion. Instead of simply thinking of what your diversity efforts might do to lift under-served or overlooked individuals, allow yourself to begin to explore how their presence will elevate the quality of your organization. Monocultural work teams lack key skills, cultural perspectives, and the wisdom that comes from di-verse lived experience. Without diverse contribution, your teams have been incomplete. However, simply including di-versity in the room does not mean your organization is ben-efiting from their full contribution. As a leader you must grow beyond simple inclusion and on to intentional empowerment by giving the teams you lead the resources, authority, and influence to lift your church, business, or community to a new level.

Lifting up, in part, includes elevating others and humbling ourselves by allowing others to elevate us. Imagine a group of people lifting one another up and allowing themselves to be lifted up. In a community of lifters, no one would feel compelled to exalt themselves. Instead it would be an environment of special honor.

ELEVATORS OF GRACE

I was at Heathrow Airport, in London, a number of years ago. When it was time for me to go from the train to the plane, I needed to move up from one floor to another. In the United States, we call lifting devices affixed in shafts in buildings "elevators." The purpose of the elevator is to lift up a person or group of people from one floor to the next. In London, however, elevators have a different name; they are called "lifts." Having stepped onto a lift, I ascended from the train level to the plane level. *How fitting an analogy!* I thought. This is exactly what my role in the lives of people, especially those on the fringes, should be. Would it not be a wonderful thing for believers to picture themselves as uplifters to help others move toward their plane in life so they can fly above their circumstances?

Practically speaking, lifting others can be done by raising a voice for those whose voice is too often ignored, silenced, or dismissed. When a children's ministry leader speaks up for the autistic and disabled community, she raises a voice for those who were not sitting at the table of decision. Who is seeking to elevate the voices of the Latinos, African Americans, Asians, females, or children at the boardroom tables in your church? Is there a family of a different culture who might be feeling excluded or invisible in your majority-race neighborhood? Could God be giving you the nudge to reach out to them and invite them over for dinner? A gracist would say, "Send me, Lord."

A WORD OF CAUTION

When attempting to be a lifter in the lives of others, please make sure that you serve others in a manner that is received by them as honoring and is not perceived as honoring only from your perspective. I can't help but think of all the times I tried to honor my wife with gifts that I thought were just perfect, only to realize that the gifts were more to my liking than hers. Yikes!

One time I bought Amber what I thought was the best gift ever. It was her birthday and I thought she would love the rice cooker I purchased. As a guy I had no idea that kitchen appliances didn't fall into the category of personal gifts. (Yes, ladies, you can laugh now.) What's worse is the year I purchased some special lingerie for my wife . . . for her birthday. I thought I was "the man." Well, you guessed it, I was acting like the man—or a typical male, I should say. I fell to the illusion that this was a great personal gift for my wife. Amber (who gave me permission to share this story with you) educated me by informing me that such gifts were really for my benefit. She actually loves to receive these kinds of gifts but would prefer them to be given when it is not her birthday. If I do desire to purchase a cooking appliance or lingerie for her birthday, I am to make sure that it is coupled with another, more personal gift that is truly for her benefit. I have learned that such gifts include a manicure, a pedicure, a spa treatment, shopping gift cards, and many other things that I've stored in my mental computer.

In Amber's mind, while my motives were right in giving her birthday gifts (okay, partially right), my method of gift giving was more self-centered than spouse-centered. Likewise, when we serve others, we must be careful to ensure that we are doing what is truly best for them and not best for us. Because our motives are often convoluted, we can psych ourselves into believing that we are lifting others up and doing good for them, when the reality is that we are looking for our own pats on the back about our advocacy, our gratification, and our desires.

I have learned that the best way to avoid such embarrassing moments is to simply ask people the best way to serve, inspire, help, or lift them.

ADOPTION VERSUS PARTNERING

My church was on a mission to minister in Kenya, Africa, and had in mind to adopt a local community where we could serve. Like many Western churches that begin work in Africa, we unfortunately began with a know-it-all attitude with our plans to clean up the neighborhood, feed the hungry, advocate for people politically, and carry out programs for the young people. Immediately after I cast a vision for reaching out to the local community we had identified, a leader pulled me aside and said, "David, we should avoid the term *adopt* and use the term *partner*." I inquired as to why, and he explained that adoption sounded like we just wanted to descend on the community as their messiah to serve them without any of their input or will. That leader was exactly right. I hadn't thought about how we were perceived or how the community in Kenya would receive our good works. Again, I was being self-centered in my attempt to lift others up without even realizing it.

After being confronted about this, I immediately changed our language and approach. I empowered our volunteers to go into the community and to the county executive's office to ask them how we could serve. We consulted the community by going door-to-door and asking people what their needs were, giving them the ownership to leverage our volunteers and money to help minister to their own community. In addition, we met with the leaders in Kenya and came alongside them to partner on reaching their villages in the best manner that they themselves prescribed. Their leaders knew exactly what was needed much better than we did. Now in Kenya the leaders of over forty churches have committed to multitribal ministry and have erected a center to serve orphans, as well as a school that we have been integral in partnering with toward success. Praise God!

SPECIAL HONORS AWARD

Buck and Big Tony, the men who make it possible for me to have a car and driver, are both behind-the-scenes servants who meet a unique and specific need. These are not the kinds of people who normally receive public praise unless they are called out and given special honor. In many ways these gentlemen have been lifters in my life. They are elevators of grace. Likewise I try my best to lift them up in ways that elevate them to higher levels of blessing in their lives.

Paul alerted us to the fact that such servants, people who may seem weaker or lesser in any way, are perfect candidates for a special honor award. These two brothers definitely qualify for the nomination of this award. And by the way, driving the pastor around is not a glorious job when you as the driver must sit in the car and wait or, worse, circle the busy streets of New York or Washington for hours until the pastor comes out of a session. This is the kind of service that the public doesn't see, but God does.

My black female entrepreneur friend, Cindy, qualifies as a candidate for the special honor award too. Others might not see the extra barriers she faces to receive capital, gain notoriety in the community, or access influential networks, but

God sees her. Such an award should be given by a committee of gracists who are seeking out hidden heroes who would never nominate themselves. My prayer is that God will lift your eyes to notice silent servants in your families, churches, and communities. By honoring them you will be honoring God.

Is it not always a beautiful thing to lift up those who are weaker, lesser known, on the outskirts of public praise, in the background of social mores, or living behind the curtains of onstage applause? Is it not the responsibility of the majority to lift up the minority? Is it not the responsibility of the stronger to lift up the weaker? Is it not required of those in power to help those who are outside of power? Would God not desire for the in-group to reach out to those who are crowded out?

LIFTING THOSE WHO FEEL CRUSHED

The Bible says, "Let someone else praise you, and not your own mouth; an outsider, and not your own lips" (Proverbs 27:2).

This proverb sets the proper order of lifting. Self-praise is discouraged, and patience to let others praise you is outlined as the prudent thing to do. But what if that affirmation never comes? What if a person continues to be overlooked? When an individual speaks up for themselves and advocates for their own value or dignity, it can sometimes be off-putting to those who don't share their same struggle and don't understand what it is like to lack the power to create change. The longer a person has felt overlooked and unheard, the stronger their words might be as they try to open the eyes and ears of others.

Just think of how it would feel to continually get passed over for a raise while working harder than your peers. Imagine seeing the lead role go to the director's daughter for the fourth time, when everyone else knows it should have gone to you. What about if your work around the house goes unnoticed by a demanding spouse, whose attention is everywhere but on the well-being of your home? What if when you finally spoke up for yourself you were met with a further dismissive response? There is something uniquely cruel about putting the pressure to remain silent on the one who is being overlooked. Unfortunately, those in the church can sometimes put more guilt on a person for not heeding this proverb that says, "Let another praise you," while at the same time absolving those in power from their responsibility to follow Paul's instruction in 1 Corinthians 12, to give special honor to those who lack it.

What would it look like if instead of dismissing the dishonored, we would honor those who have been dismissed? When African Americans began to lift up the cry that Black Lives Matter it was met with an unsympathetic counter from many white Americans that further dismissed the pain these brothers and sisters were experiencing. Many white evangelical Americans did not take the lead from their black brothers and sisters, but instead replied with "all lives matter" and disparaged the phrase "black lives matter" because of ideological differences with organizational founders. I wonder how the movement would have looked different if white Americans would have been early adopters to elevate the affirmation that the lives of black people not only matter but should receive special honor in their time of pain. What do you think would have happened if the white community would have lifted up their own voices and actions with strength, sincerity, and sacrifice to declare that "Black Lives Matter"? What would that have done to build bridges of reconciliation across uniquely pain-filled racial lines?

When a person or community is consistently disempowered it should not be surprising that they feel compelled to lift up the only thing they continue to have power over: their voice.

In other venues we know the value of having someone else lift us up in the presence of others. For anyone creating content on social media for their new business, they know personally what it feels like when a friend hypes them up and shares their posts. For someone out in the dating field, having a wingman who talks you up to that potential date they just met is invaluable. When we're looking for a job, a personal recommendation from a friend seems to move our résumé to the top of the stack. I even wonder if those who struggle with interjecting themselves into conversations at parties, and those who feel the need to be self-promotional, are doing so because we fail to recognize their contributions. What would happen if we were to release a force of encouragers—gracists, if you will—and people who were radically inclusive? Can you imagine what would happen if those on the sidelines of popularity and preferences, and those who are culturally overpowered, were actually valued, included, and inspired to join the ranks of the celebrated? What would happen to their spirits of discouragement, depression, and disillusionment?

My guess is that walls of separation between our churches would shatter. I believe that people would not have to fight for themselves if we would stand up for one another. Racially speaking, I would love to see white, black, Asian, and Latino churches become elevators of grace to one another. It would do my heart good to see churches wash the feet of one another across denominational and racial lines. Would it not bless the heart of God to see his multicultural family of believers commit to lifting up each other on purpose, with purpose, for a divine purpose? In so doing we will not only bless God and each other, but we will also not abandon those who stand alone in self-advocacy, lifting their voices for change hoping that someone will echo back that they not only matter, but deserve special honor.

WHEN THE WALLS COME DOWN

Once the walls come down, we still have to live together. This is where the rubber meets the road. How are we to live together when the melting pot of black, white, Latino, Arab, Asian, young, old, rich, poor, Democrat, Republican, blue and white collar all converge—or crash—in the same church? It is sometimes true that when the walls come down the gloves come off. Sometimes exposure to different cultures, styles, and preferences may clash with one's personal likes and dislikes. What happens when the elevator gets crowded? Multicultural ministry takes real work, as we will discover in the next several chapters.

5

Saying Two:
I WILL COVER YOU

The parts that are unpresentable are treated
with special modesty, while our presentable
parts need no special treatment.

1 Corinthians 12:23-24 (Emphasis Added)

Modesty is a term that could carry a lot of baggage, depending on what Christian circles you run in. For many, the very subjective teachings on modesty from church leaders have laid a heavy burden of man-made requirements on our sisters in Christ. We normally frame the application of any teaching on the concept of modesty solely around the limits and freedoms of dress that a woman is pressured to stick to; all with the intent to temper the sexual urges of men. Can you even remember a time you heard a sermon on modesty that didn't include a teaching that centered on cautioning women to watch how they dress? The church has used the weight of its spiritual leadership to comment on how low this neckline can be, how high that hemline should be, and how formfitting clothing can be to be considered appropriate. Some people reading this passage in 1 Corinthians might read this phrase "special modesty" and immediately start thinking back to their church's teaching on purity. Even though we will be talking about covering, clothing, and modesty, this time our conversation on this topic will be different.

In this passage, when speaking about the different parts of the body, the biblical author acknowledges that people are known to have certain aspects of their own body that they do not want to be on display for the world to see. The author calls these parts "unpresentable." Let's not assume these parts are determined to be unpresentable because of society's or church leaders' standards. Instead, it is under the agency and preference of the individual to not want certain parts to be presented to the world. They personally decide what to keep covered and unpresented. If a part of the body that a person wishes to keep covered becomes exposed, there can be a feeling of unwelcome vulnerability. A covering when a person feels exposed can bring protection and security. A covering at a time like that can shield the vulnerable from embarrassment or harm. There is a certain respect that is given to another person when they are afforded the dignity of being seen as they wish and not being caught unguarded or exposed against their will. Special modesty then, in this passage, is a grace given to an individual in order to affirm their dignity and present their body in the way they wish that does not broadcast their vulnerabilities to the world.

MY SWAG

Everyone who knows me knows that I love the swag that I've got, especially when it comes to my fashion. I try to look my freshest when I walk out of the door. I'm always on the lookout for the drip (for you folks that are unaware, that's just another word for *outfit*) that is right for me. So, when I met a seamstress in Kenya who told me she could make me clothes that actually fit my body, I got really excited. She took my measurements, and she asked how I liked certain styles and colors. In a couple of weeks when I got to try on these custom-made clothes, I couldn't wait to see how I looked. When I put on the suit she made me and I matched it with the right watch, glasses, and shoes, I couldn't have been more pleased with how I looked.

That's the thing about the clothes we wear; they give us the ability to present our best side while strategically covering the vulnerabilities, blemishes, embarrassing spots, and weaker assets we wish to be kept private.

Likewise the body of Christ needs to learn how to offer that same grace of covering to the parts of the spiritual body that request it. In fact, Paul wrote to the Colossians that they were to clothe themselves with "compassion, kindness, humility, gentleness and patience" (Colossians 3:12). These behaviors and attitudes that Paul mentions in Colossians are the attributes that body members ought to have toward each other across racial, ethnic, and class lines. At first you may think I'm stretching the meaning of the verse, but notice the verse that leads to the above statement about clothing the body: "Here there is no Gentile or Jew, circumcised or uncircumcised, barbarian, Scythian, slave or free, but Christ is all, and is in all" (Colossians 3:11). Do you notice that Paul mentions race, religious practice, ethnicity, and class in verse 11? Then to top off the message, he begins verse 12 with the word *therefore*, meaning "based on what I have just stated in the previous verses." So the verse reads like this: "Therefore, as God's chosen people, holy and dearly loved, clothe yourselves with compassion, kindness, humility, gentleness and patience."

The call to cover one another is the call to express godly attitudes before judging or exposing areas of the body that are blemished or unseemly. When you and I are hurt by another part of the body, we are to handle it in a way that is clothed with the aforementioned attitudes and behaviors. There are some vulnerable issues in the body of Christ and even among our cultural, racial, and denominational groups that need to be dealt with behind closed doors in a healthy manner. I don't say this to imply that the church should sweep sin under the rug or refuse to address matters of immorality or abuse. That can only lead to more sin and abuse. My point is that we must not air the dirty laundry immediately, especially as it relates to race.

Modesty in the way we speak about ethnic groups, genders, and classes is critical to unity. While we may want to blast a particular group within the body of Christ because we disagree with their theology, methodology, politics, or philosophy of ministry, it may behoove us to reconsider how we speak about them. We must ensure that we have the clothing of grace on to cover with dignity parts of our body that are vulnerable and blemished.

TAKING AIM

I remember one author whose material I read in Bible college and who seemed to want to take aim at every part of the body of Christ that didn't agree with his own biblical view. When he criticized the various parts of the body without the clothing of grace on, it became hurtful and divisive. A pastor friend of mine was a victim of this author's attack. While the author's book took aim at the style of ministry my pastor friend was leading, I don't believe the author realized that he was being careless and divisive. When my pastor friend was asked in a staff meeting whether he was going to write a book or article to retort, he responded by saying, "There is nothing the devil would like to see more than two high-profile Christian leaders publicly fighting. I will not be used that way, and the non-Christian world would be distracted by that kind of testimony." I was impressed by this mature response. I can also tell you that my pastor friend and another Christian leader sat down with the author behind closed doors to address the matters in search of reconciliation.

The principle is this: when you or I have the power to criticize another denomination, ministry, class, or group, let's not take aim and fire. Let's power down and cover the body of Christ with compassion, kindness, humility, gentleness, and patience. Attitudes and behaviors such as these will lead us down the road to reconciliation much faster.

Paul continues in Colossians 3:13-14 to encourage forbearance and forgiveness, followed up by love to cover all the virtues so that perfect unity will be the result. Perfect unity involves the areas of difference listed in verse 11, which include but are not limited to race, ethnicity, religious rituals, and class.

SPECIAL MODESTY

Paul's words about clothing in the book of Colossians shed light on the importance of his message about modesty in 1 Corinthians. The apostle said that those who are "unpresentable" should be covered with special modesty. This means that there are times when those who aren't the popular race or church or powerful class may need to be covered, shielded, or advocated for. There are times when it would be easy for those who are more powerful and popular to use their capabilities to embarrass the dignity of those who would otherwise be easily exposed. This is what the unwise author I spoke about earlier did to my pastor friend, as well as many other victims in his sights, including groups like charismatic Christians, Christian counselors, and the contemporary worship movement within churches across North America. I believe it is incumbent upon those with power or privilege to take on the responsibility to protect and cover those who don't have them.

The question is, if people watched how we treated each other's vulnerabilities, would they describe our actions with words like care, protect, and safeguard? May we never be comfortable saying, "I don't care what the Methodist church down the street does; they are not my denomination" or "I don't care what the white church five miles away does; they are not my spiritual siblings." I believe that such statements would horrify Christ. Do we do this regarding race and class? Do we say about those who are poor, "Oh well, they made their bed; now they must sleep in it." May it never be!

You see, friends, if we don't care about each other, then we will not cover each other.

Just think of the discretion and seriousness with which you would handle the situation if your teenage child was having a personal struggle. To what degree do I as a parent share the details of my child's personal business with anyone but my spouse? One's child needs to be covered too, right? He or she needs the dignity of privacy and special modesty. There are ways for a parent to seek advice from others without embarrassing their child in the public gaze. So with the same care that a parent would have with their child, let us cover one another with modesty.

Paul said that there are those among us who need special modesty. Gracism demands that we take those who are marginalized as minorities and ensure that they are covered and protected from embarrassment where possible.

Can you imagine a visitor attending a church and tripping down the aisle on the way in? That would be embarrassing. Now imagine that later in the service someone from the stage, such as the worship leader or pastor, refers to the tripping spell in a joking way. That would be cold, heartless, and embarrassing humor at the expense of the guest. Not cool, right? Now consider if the person is not only a visitor but is one of a mere five Asian people in a gathering of a couple hundred people. Courtesy would require that we refrain from leveling humor at someone else's expense anyway. Hospitality, however, would require that we bend over backward to help a guest. Gracism demands even more. Gracism requires that I increase my sensitivity level to the guest because of his minority status, understanding that he is also unofficially representing other Asians by virtue of association, whether spoken or unspoken, welcome or unwelcome, fair or unfair. It is the reality of being in the minority position and is the weight carried by many. Just as Christians carry the weight of their testimony as Christ-followers and represent, whether officially or unofficially, their Lord and the reputation of others who call themselves Christians, so minorities carry with them the weight of those they represent.

THE EMBARRASSMENT FACTOR

In light of this, what is special modesty? It is the special sensitivity toward minorities in whatever form they may come to this status—white, black, visitors, foreigners, religious, marginalized, disabled, nonassertive, and so on—to ensure that their reputations and dignity are taken into account before (if ever) their weaknesses, blemishes, or vulnerabilities are exposed.

The point I am emphasizing is that those who are in the minority position have a higher potential for embarrassment due to their status. For instance, if a white male finds himself in a gathering that is populated by a majority of African American females, he is vulnerable to a greater level of embarrassment than if he were in a homogeneous white environment. Therefore, it is the responsibility of the gracist to ensure that he is protected, covered, and cared for with extra grace that may not be required for others in the room. Gracists take on the job of caring for the marginalized regardless of their color, class, or culture. They intentionally reach out to those who are on the fringe, and if for some reason the marginalized person or group falters, gracism demands covering that person in such a way that his dignity is protected and his faults are not exploited.

How different would your life be if you lived each day committed to the dignity of those around you, especially those in need of extra care? What would such a day look like in your world? Instead of families, communities, and churches being filled with backbiting or suspicion, how about them being places where believers seek to help each other look and feel their best? How about an environment where I seek to help you succeed and you seek to encourage me? Or more, if I fall or fail, will you exploit and embarrass me because you can, or will you cover me? Is there not a balance somewhere between my sanctification and my missteps? If I ask the wrong question, use the wrong racial language, or hold an unpopular social view, will you call me a racist or sexist, or will you cover me while inspiring me to new levels of education and growth? These questions are poignant because they get to the heart of what it means to cover others who haven't been fully enlightened or sanctified.

Like a child who needs protection, so too many people in the maturation process of race relations also need room to struggle, grow, disagree, and fail. The principle of covering people or giving them this space to mature in matters of reconciliation is extremely important to the safety of their process, lest their multicultural growth be stunted.

Paul exhorted the believers in Corinth to offer special modesty to those on the outer rings of social and cultural acceptability. In order to live out the kind of lifestyle that suppresses our human desire to gossip, slander, put down, and expose the weaknesses and faults of others, Paul lobbies for a new kind of faith expression—one where care and concern for the reputation of the minority, or the weaker one, is taken into account.

6

Saying Three:
I WILL SHARE WITH YOU

The parts that are unpresentable are treated
with special modesty, while our presentable
parts need no special treatment.

1 CORINTHIANS 12:23-24 (EMPHASIS ADDED)

I was flying home from England with a good friend, Roger, whom I had been traveling with across the world to build bridges of reconciliation. We were on a major airline, and all had gone smoothly in our travels from Africa to Europe. But in London it became apparent that there was a mix-up with our tickets. I was ticketed for economy, which was the way it was supposed to be, and Roger's ticket was clearly for business class on this final leg from London to Baltimore. Because of administrative errors, Roger's itinerary in the airline computer stated that he was to be seated in the economy class with me. After speaking to the counter worker, Roger was told that he could take a later flight on which the airline would correct the error, so that he could sit in the comfort of business class. The only other option was for

Roger to sit in economy class, where he would be squeezed in with the rest of us.

COMFORT OR COMMUNITY?

What would you do? Put yourself in Roger's shoes where you have the privilege to upgrade and take another flight that would get you home in about the same amount of time. You have the status, the history, the airline points accumulated, and the right to ride in a more comfortable class. The only downside is that you would not be able to fly with your associate. You would lose the opportunity to share in fellowship with your friend. You would get to experience the comforts of the nicer class but would do so alone. What choice would you make in this scenario? What did Roger do?

To my surprise, Roger chose to ride with me in economy for the seven-hour journey. He wasn't happy about the mistake the airline had made, but he was pleased to ride with me. The choice seemed easy for him once he got over his frustration at the airline's error coming at the end of a long trip. Once Roger gathered his thoughts and made a value judgment between comfort and community, he chose community. Roger would rather fly with his friend than fly alone. The comforts of flying solo didn't override his desire for community and companionship.

The apostle Paul said, "The parts that are unpresentable are treated with special modesty, while our presentable parts need *no special treatment*" (1 Corinthians 12:23-24, emphasis added). While special modesty says "I will cover you," the phrase *no special treatment* says, "I refuse to accept favors or perks that may hurt you," even if the refusal is emotionally difficult. If my choice to express my rights, freedoms, and privileges will chip away at your dignity, then I will think twice about exercising that right in that moment. This does not mean that I cannot enjoy the privileges and luxuries of life, but it does take into account how and when I enjoy those privileges and luxuries. If my acceptance of special favors makes you feel put down or less dignified, then I'll pass on the favor and share in your experience.

The third saying of Paul in 1 Corinthians 12 may be the hardest principle of gracism to accept, because it cuts to the heart of our insatiable appetite for entitlement and the expression of individual freedom. The concept of downshifting, downgrading, or refusing to accept special treatment is antithetical to Western individualism and assaults much of what we have been taught as being our inalienable rights. Downgrading in order to share in community is countercultural to upward mobility and personal aggrandizement.

While I am in no way arguing for communism, I am saying that when you and I have a choice to either share in community or enjoy special treatment that would leave others out, we are put into a quandary. Such intersections can be dealt with in only one of two ways. Either "I will lift you up," as the first saying goes, or "I will share with you" in community, as the third saying proclaims.

Often sharing is defined as giving a part of what I have to someone else who doesn't have it. If you are hungry and I have a slice of bread, then sharing would be me giving a piece of my bread to you so that you, too, can eat.

I sense that the nuance of sharing Paul was speaking about in this passage is the sharing of common experiences. It is not simply giving cash to those in the body who do not have. Rather, it is majority persons refusing to accept special treatment, perks, and honors that are unnecessary in the face of those who do not have them. Accepting such "in-your-face" special treatment is the opposite of humility and grace. Though it may feel good to be special and above the rest, power and prestige can be addictive drugs that rob others of life's basics.

SHARING AS AN ANTIDOTE TO POLARIZATION

What does this act of sharing look like for those in this world who are decision makers? If you are a parent, policy maker, manager, partner, or serve in some other role of leadership, you have a special position that affords you the power to give the final word on decisions that affect the lives of others. Delivering an extra measure of grace to refuse autonomy in order to be collaborative can mean the world to those in your sphere of influence. The special privileges that your position provides allow you to push your agenda, have things your way, set the culture, and limit the influence of others. How much more dynamic it is when a person with a formal role of authority does not steamroll others with the weight of their position.

A veteran chief of staff for a congressman spoke to one of my associates recently and commented on the changes he's seen on Capitol Hill over the past decade. He reflected on how it used to be the case that if a bill came up for a vote, both parties would collaborate back and forth to negotiate to have aspects of the written law be favorable to the constituents of each side. Even though the majority party could force a new policy to only favor their agenda, they chose to cultivate collaboration across the aisle. He said, "You never knew when the power would shift, so you didn't want to ruin your chances to have them be favorable to you in the future." He went on to say that collaboration like that has now been replaced by the polarization of today. The current political divide is such that whichever party, no matter Republican or Democrat, holds the majority seats gives up nothing and further alienates those they once would have worked with.

Being in the majority gives decision makers special privileges. Just because we can get our way doesn't mean it is best to get our way by any means necessary. What if each of us, when we make decisions that have implications for others, refuse the special privilege of unilateral authority and, instead, invite collaboration with those who share different perspectives, views, and interests than our own? And what if we refuse to resort to coercing others into submission to our ways using the excuse that the ends justify the means? What if we redefine success as leaders to require some measure of togetherness rather than simply getting our way? We can actively push back against polarization through gracist decision making that "shares with" one another.

GETTING A PIECE OF THE PIE

Imagine a line of church members waiting to get a plate of food at a church dinner. Let's say there are fifty members and five guests. Because the members know where the food is, know the process of getting the food, and know the house rules, they have the advantage of eating first. They also know that there are typically not enough desserts at these monthly functions. Most of the insiders are aware of this and have come up with a system to ensure that they get their piece of the pie. While getting their meal in line, they have the cook in the back set aside some pie for them in the kitchen. When it's time for dessert, the five guests who are unaware of the inside information lose out on getting any pie.

What happened here? The insiders—majority persons— had the knowledge and networks to make the system of attaining dessert work in their favor. There was no crime committed, no one hurt physically or financially, no massive act of discrimination levied against the visitors. The uninformed guests simply didn't get to enjoy a piece of the pie because the majority players had inside knowledge and received special treatment.

1 CORINTHIANS 11

While the illustration I gave above is a modern-day example of how people on the fringes of community can be left out, Paul builds the concepts of gracism on real-life examples that came out of the divided church in Corinth. In chapter 11, Paul rebukes the Corinthians for discriminating against those who had no inside knowledge or favor. He brings correction on the majority for enjoying food with special treatment while others were last in line, and some didn't get to eat at the church dinner at all. The greedy appetites of the in-group failed to include those of the out-group.

Here is Paul's criticism toward the Corinthians in his own words.

> When you come together, it is not the Lord's Supper you eat, for when you are eating, some of you go ahead with your own private suppers. As a result, one person remains hungry and another gets drunk. Don't you have homes to eat and drink in? Or do you despise the church of God by humiliating those who have nothing? What shall I say to you? Shall I praise you? Certainly not in this matter! (1 Corinthians 11:20-22)

Notice that Paul is upset because those who did not have as much were being humiliated by the freedoms of those who clearly could enjoy the luxury of fine dining at home in private. Paul is not rebuking the Corinthians because of their privileges and luxuries at home, but because of their failure to commune with the less fortunate. Paul is preaching that the privileged ones need no special treatment, but the ones in the body who do not have luxuries have to be included purposefully at the table of Communion lest they be left out. Paul's solution was not for the Corinthians to refrain from enjoying Communion and fellowship around the table. His solution was gracism through the art of inclusion. Notice what he wrote: "So then, my brothers and sisters, when you gather to eat, you should all eat together. Anyone who is hungry should eat something at home, so that when you meet together it may not result in judgment" (1 Corinthians 11:33-34).

Discernment and inclusion are so important in the body of Christ that Paul would rather the more privileged folks eat at home before coming to the church fellowship dinner, so that those with empty stomachs could feast on more of the community food.

A PIECE OF PIE FOR THE OUTSIDERS

Remember the five visitors who didn't get any pie at the church dinner? How would a gracist in the group of fifty insiders act differently? A gracist in the majority group would either refuse the special treatment of having pie held back in the kitchen or would make certain that the outsiders were offered a piece of the pie before it was all gone. This is a clear example of looking out for those who don't have the privileged position or are on the fringes. Sharing the pie brings joy and fellowship to everyone.

Does this mean that special treatment is always wrong? No, not always. It is wrong only when it damages community, companionship, or social mores. When my perks cause you pain or loss, then, like Paul said, "our presentable parts need no special treatment" (1 Corinthians 12:24). Do I want special treatment? Of course I do. My flesh loves the world and all its goodies. But the body is coordinated by the Spirit of God and not by the flesh. Therefore what I want and what I need are two distinct things. Do I need special treatment? No. Paul said the presentable parts—the majority persons, the insiders—do not "need" special treatment. In fact it is the visitor who needs the special treatment (gracism) so that he or she can partake in what others commonly enjoy.

Paul's point is that I should be willing to share in your common experience for the sake of unity or be willing to lift you up to my status in order for us to share in community. Refusing special favors in the face of others is a difficult concept to grasp because it seemingly argues against all I've earned and worked for. But please understand that I am not saying, nor do I believe Paul meant, that accomplishing and earning are wrong. There will always be different classes of people and various levels of status within churches and other communities. I believe, however, that gracism is the equalizer that will allow those of higher status to relate to those of lower status. The gracist who says "I will share with you" is willing to sit in the home of a person whose home is not as nice for dinner instead of always hosting the meal. Sharing, beyond giving of what I have, can be the willingness to commune with others on their turf, at their home, in their part of the airplane. It can mean that I lay aside my prerogatives to enter another's reality.

Could Jesus not have availed himself of the accoutrements of heaven when coming to earth? Sure, he could have. Yet Jesus chose to lay aside his divine prerogatives to dwell among mortals (Philippians 2:5-11). It was in that dwelling that fellowship and union took place. Jesus was willing to share in the commonality of our human experience. When was the last time you shared with someone in this way—shared in their experience, on their turf, in their world?

GRACEONOMICS

As a man, I receive benefits and prerogatives that women do not. For example, I can usually get a better deal when purchasing a vehicle than do many women. While this is not a universal rule, past studies have shown discrimination in the car sales industry when it comes to gender. So am I to refuse a good deal and pay more money for a vehicle than I have to in the name of gracism? No way. When my gracist nature must kick in, however, is when I know that a female friend is looking to purchase a vehicle. I should step alongside her to ensure that she gets a good deal. Maybe I ask if she might let me negotiate for her. Maybe on her behalf I call in one of my favors to a car dealer friend, ensuring that she receives the same treatment I was afforded. But I must do something. I cannot sit by and receive special treatment while she gets ripped off.

This kind of fight for justice must happen not simply on the personal level but systemically as well. When I become aware of others who are not being treated fairly while I'm being given special treatment, that should give pause inside of me to refuse my special status and make right what is wrong in a systemic way through advocacy for causes that defy injustice.

Does gracism, as it relates to special treatment, prevent me from purchasing a nice home while others in the church live in trailers? Again, practically speaking, I cannot solve the financial gaps among people by purchasing homes for everyone in the church. I can, however, ensure that the person looking to buy a home is not being discriminated against when looking to get a bank loan for a new home. I can open doors to my network of loan officers and mortgage brokers who will bend over backward to do me a favor after my history of business with them.

I call this *graceonomics*. It is the leveraging of financial and relational networks to help others succeed in their economic worlds. Assisting people in achieving financial success and reaching their educational and economic potential is a joy for me, especially when they may not have had the same opportunities, breaks, or luck I have had. Graceonomics are acts of gracism as they relate to money, class, opportunity, and justice. Such acts are at the heart of reconciliation.

Whether church dinners, cars, homes, airline flights, or other scenarios, the point is the same. There are those who are "unpresentable" (minorities, dotted, outsiders, on-the-fringe folks) who are in need of special treatment when I, the presentable one, am not. Therefore it is my Christian responsibility (which is different from my inalienable right as a human being) to refuse upgrades in the face of my brother or sister. I must either help the "unpresentable" ones to upgrade with me or share with them in their experience of lack. Otherwise I may get seduced by entitlements and become addicted to the prestige that comes with power—all of which can be gained on the backs or in the face of others who don't have the same insider information and networks that I've been afforded.

My friend Roger and I had a blast in economy class. Yes, we were crunched, but we shared in the experience—one of many crazy memories we enjoy. While Roger could have sat in business class, he chose community instead. Paul said that we were baptized by one Spirit and given one Spirit to drink (1 Corinthians 12:13). In this oneness we must figure out how we are to live together without one group putting down another while the other is elevated. The solution is gracism. A community of gracists is a group of believers who are crazy enough to believe that God's unifying Spirit is increasingly active among those who choose to lift each other up, cover one another, and refuse special favors in the face of others who are on the fringes.

Gracist living doesn't refuse the good things that life has to offer. It simply refuses to ignore those who aren't as privileged to enjoy such benefits and is committed to doing something about it.

GRACEONOMICS BRIDGING POLITICAL DIVIDES

In recent years, I have begun experiencing the joy of letting my passion for generosity and giving become a team sport. I recognized that there were a number of people in my network who shared my delight in taking part in similar acts of generosity. I decided to put out the call to about a dozen folks to meet together regularly to pray for and encourage one another in leveling up our giving. Now this wasn't just about writing more checks. This was about infusing generous living and generous giving into our everyday lives.

I developed a unique friendship with one of the members of this generosity group. He's a young African American business executive named Kevin. He and I would connect throughout the week and he would regularly tell me how God would meet him with a unique word or "giving challenge" during his morning runs. It wasn't uncommon for him to reach out to me and say something like, "Pastor, God is giving me a nudge to be on the lookout to give to a woman who is a widow" or "I just got a bonus at work and I sensed God telling me that he wants me to bless someone who is experiencing a crisis in their life." It became a regular occurrence for me to hear from Kevin in the morning and meet someone who fit that demographic later on that day.

One morning, after one of these famous runs, Kevin reached out to tell me that he had been praying through his frustration around the hurt and pain he was feeling as a black man during a season of racially tense political leadership. He felt and knew that the division he was sensing was getting to him and he didn't want it to win. He told me that he felt like God was telling him to give to a person who was on the other side of the political aisle from him, as a way to build a bridge of gracism.

Not long after that, a man named Bob called into the daily radio talk show I host here in the nation's capital. Bob was a political firecracker and he fit the bill exactly with his brash party-line talking points. He was very robust in his strong opinions on racial and political matters. When Kevin listened to the clip from the show I sent him, he said it was a bull's-eye. Kevin even said that it was a good thing he had some time to cool down because he needed God's grace to wash over him before he could pray with Bob.

Before Bob and I finished our call on the radio show, I asked him what I could pray for him about and he told me that he was experiencing financial difficulties. He and his wife had to move back into his parents' house, and he was struggling to pay the bills. I got his info so we could follow up.

Kevin and I set up a video call with Bob so that we could engage a little more and pray for him. After some genuine conversation and taking some time to pray together, Kevin told Bob about the financial gift and that he wanted to take care of four months of car payments for Bob. He communicated that this was a gift from the Lord and that "Even though we disagree on a lot, we do agree on one thing and that is Christ is our Savior, and because of that we are called to take care of each other and love each other." This gift expressed not only our love, care, and concern for Bob but also the Lord's care during his time of need.

It would be an understatement to say the man was blown away by this type of generosity. The bridge was built and grace-onomics proved to connect the parts of the body that had faced incredible pressures of division.

What made this gift a bridge-building gift is that it was personal, it was intentional, and it was inspired by the Lord. I wonder what kind of healing could take place across some of our deepest divides if more gifts were given in this way. This gift did not change anyone's mind about votes and it didn't change the hurt that can come from political leaders and political decisions that adversely affect the people group we represent. But what it did do was remind both sides about the dignity and humanity and interdependence that exists among all parts of the body.

My friend Kevin and I began to have so many generosity encounters like this that we started *The Graceonomics Podcast* where we share story after story of generous living and generous giving. I'm sure you tech-savvy readers will be able to find it out there on the web. Wouldn't it be powerful to see a movement of graceonomics and to hear of generosity groups springing up around the world that intentionally leverage the grace of giving to be an extension of God's love and care for this broken and hurting world?

The art of inclusion is the ability to reach out to those who are on the fringes and those on the opposite side of some of our most overwhelming ideological divides. It is the extension of radical inclusivity to those who may not have the education, networks, or breaks in life that I have had. It is inviting them in to enjoy the fruits of my world. Is this not what Jesus Christ did for us as our premier example of sharing?

7

Saying Four:
I WILL HONOR YOU

God has put the body together, giving greater
honor *to the parts that lacked it.*

1 Corinthians 12:24 (Emphasis Added)

Do you remember the mathematical equations you learned in school that had symbols attached to them? Remember the greater-than (>) and less-than (<) symbols? Once a number was assigned to each side of the symbol, the elementary student was asked to choose which number was greater than or less than the other. While I never really enjoyed mathematics, I could achieve average scores with the greater-than and less-than symbols.

Our heavenly Father values us all, but he is clearly a gracist when it comes to his divine equations. Notice who Paul said God honors when he combines people and assigns the greater-than value of honor to people. Paul states in 1 Corinthians 12:24 that "God has put the body together, giving greater honor to the parts that lacked it."

I find it unsettling to think that God would put a multi-cultural, multieconomical, multigifted, and multidimensional group of believers together and then assign a greater-than symbol to some of the people. Yet he does. Why? And to whom does he assign the greater-than sign?

From Paul's statement it seems that God does not assign greater honor to those with certain gifts, economic status, or even ethnicity, although some may argue that Paul was speaking of Gentiles here. It seems to me that the writer was clearly stating that those who have "lacked it" (honor) are the ones who have qualified for greater honor. Those groups who have come with honor deficits are first in line for greater honor from heaven's perspective.

THE FAIRNESS FACTOR

Do you know anyone who is honor deficient? These are people who lack what the majority enjoy. People within the Christian body and outside it who live in lack may qualify for honors they did not earn if we follow Paul's logic in this passage. The normal way of life for those in North America, generally speaking, is one lived on the system of earnings, right? Basically, if one works, one earns money. If one achieves, one is awarded. It is that simple. If you do not achieve or work for your earnings, then you fall short of honor and the normal rewards that come with accomplishment. This seems fair and right.

The problem with grace is that it is unfair. Why should a homeless person or welfare recipient receive my hard-earned money if he or she chooses not to work? Have you ever thought this? I have. Admittedly this is not the most compassionate attitude, but at the same time the alarm on my fairness meter loudly sounds, "Unfair, unjust, foul." What about the work I've done? What about the investment of time, effort, energy, money, risk, and faith it took for me to get to this level of life? What about the extra efforts I at times have had to make as an African American in the United States to overcome real and perceived odds?

Whenever I have found myself thinking like this, I have been reminded by the Spirit of God that I would be nothing if it were not for Christ. You have heard the saying "If not for the grace of God, there go I." That phrase settles the sounds of my fairness meter quickly. It takes only a few minutes of reflection on Psalm 103 to reorient me.

> The LORD is compassionate and gracious,
>   slow to anger, abounding in love.
> He will not always accuse,
>   nor will he harbor his anger forever;
> he does not treat us as our sins deserve
>   or repay us according to our iniquities.
>   (Psalm 103:8-10)

The words that say "he does not treat us as our sins deserve" are the ones that are etched into my mind. God really is not fair. Grace is not fair. Theologians often argue for the justice of God based on the death of Christ. I agree that the justice requirement for our sin debt has been satisfied through the substitutionary atonement of Jesus Christ. But that still isn't fair. Justice may have been served, but Jesus still suffered for sins he did not commit. While it is true that God the Father is satisfied with the moral payment, do any of us believe that Jesus got a fair deal?

I can't rejoice over the sufferings of Christ on my behalf. It breaks me up. It makes me weep to think of the price my Savior paid. My redemption was invaluable. Reflecting on it is evoking an emotional response even as I write this line. It is not fair. Jesus got a bum deal.

The reality is that we are all bums who have not earned one thing we enjoy. If you have an education, it is because God blessed you to get it. If you are smart and can think with a clear mind, it is because God blessed you with a brain that works. If you are athletic, the use of your limbs is a gift. The air we breathe is a gift. When I begin to think like this, I am reminded that, spiritually speaking, I was a beggar on the side of life's road when Jesus gave me the bread of life to eat, living water to drink, and clothes of redemption to wear.

BANQUET AND BUMS

Jesus explained the concept of honor when he told the parable of the banquet. The table of honor was occupied by those who placed themselves at the most distinguished seats. Notice Jesus' advice for those who seek to be honored by others and not be self-promoting.

> When he noticed how the guests picked the places of honor at the table, he told them this parable: "When someone invites you to a wedding feast, do not take the place of honor, for a person more distinguished than you may have been invited. If so, the host who invited both of you will come and say to you, 'Give this person your seat.' Then, humiliated, you will have to take the least important place. But when you are invited, take the lowest place, so that when your host comes, he will say to you, 'Friend, move up to a better place.' Then you will be honored in the presence of all the other guests. For all those who exalt themselves will be humbled, and those who humble themselves will be exalted." (Luke 14:7-11)

God is in the exalting business and loves to honor his servants. He will give even greater honor to those who lack it most. When continuing to read Luke 14, we see that Jesus took the parable to another level as he explained the great wedding banquet. Because the invited ones (alluding to a majority of the Jewish people) rejected their invitation to salvation through Jesus Christ as the Messiah, the banquet host ordered his servants, "Go out quickly into the streets and alleys of the town and bring in the poor, the crippled, the blind and the lame" (Luke 14:21).

Who are the ones who lack honor and deserve a greater measure of it? In heaven's eyes it is the poor, crippled, blind, and lame. That's right, the lower class, the outcast, the marginalized, the poor, and disabled. It is these who have honor deficits that are made greater.

In this parable, Jesus is putting privilege on display. He is not just acknowledging the existence of social privilege, he is highlighting how those who have it often do not recognize how it can be used for kingdom impact. The greater one's awareness is of the different ways they carry a higher level of perceived honor by the standards of this world, the greater opportunity they have to intentionally sacrifice that privilege to give greater honor to others. Our self-awareness and social-awareness of these privilege-awarding qualities are an essential aspect of how we identify moments where we can join God in his exalting business. This means if you are in the in-group, it is not for your benefit alone. If you are considered distinguished by others, don't let it go to your head. If you have a social privilege based on being in the majority group, use it to bring greater honor to those who others exclude, dismiss, or treat poorly.

This parable is an example, straight from Jesus, of how one individual has the power to upend exclusive social and structural norms. One person who joins the Lord in the "exalting business" is able to leverage their own privilege to show the true value of those that the world might marginalize. But if each of us is caught up in our own self-advancement and fighting to get the best seat we have access to, we are not only missing an opportunity to honor someone else, we are setting ourselves up for the humbling hand of the Lord.

The poor and the crippled do not have the privilege that allows them to walk into a prepared banquet. They must be sought after and retrieved. Greater honor is given to them by God. Initiation from the banquet hosts to search the streets for the less honorable is the representation of what God has done for each of us. You and I are the poor in spirit, the morally crippled, the spiritually blind, and the emotionally lame people on the streets of sin and darkness. God, in his grace, has sent out the great host of heaven, Jesus Christ, and his servants to proclaim the good news that an undeserved banquet has been prepared. Unbelievable, isn't it? Why would we ever choose to miss an opportunity to use our privilege to give that same honor to others around us?

Earlier I said that it is unsettling to me that God would extend greater honor to some. That is the effect of grace, though. It is unsettling and unfair, and yet divine. I now believe it is okay to be unfair, not for the purposes of hurting others, but for the purposes of helping those who are in a state of lack. This kind of unfairness—gracism, if you will—is not only okay, it is commanded. Therefore, as a converted gracist, I must, like God, be an extender of grace and honor to everyone. Moreover, I must give greater honor to the ones who lack it most.

How? In five ways: service, speech, social media, stewardship, and sitting.

SERVICE

It honors God when I serve the poor, the crippled, the blind, and the lame. The brokenness of this world determines that qualities like these indicate that a person is less valuable, when in fact God does not look at any of these qualities when determining someone's value. Their value is high in God's sight, but their social honor has been made low by man. It is in this disparity that we find a prime opportunity to leverage any advantage we might have in order to highlight that which the world has missed. When anyone has an honor deficit, regardless of color or class, it is my duty as a gracist to reach out and serve that person.

If you are a Puerto Rican, can you see yourself serving someone who is Mexican? If you are an American citizen, can you see yourself serving first generation immigrants? Even if you are against illegal immigration and support political action to build a wall at our southern border, when the human need for food, clothing, or medical care confronts your community, are you willing to serve the human beings on your doorstep?

I remember when a vote came up on a foundation board that I served on a number of years ago. The vote was regarding donating money to an organization that would care for the human needs of Latinos in my community. A leader within the community had the calling and vision to minister to the human needs of Latinos and was requesting funds to do so. While deliberating the request, I had internal questions, as well as some open ones, about whether we were perpetuating illegal immigration by serving this foreign-born people group. Thinking personally about the people I encountered, helped, related to, and entertained in my home felt different to me than this decision. My personal care for human needs required one aspect of gracism, but now I was being asked to institutionalize the caring of foreign-born humans on a broader systemic basis.

After much consideration and thought I realized that without systemic change I could never influence greater numbers of people to receive the personal care that I afforded to a few. I now had the opportunity with one vote to help thousands of Latinos without making their legal status a qualification for my service. My conviction about the human need issue, whether legal or not, was solidified by Jesus' words to feed and care for the "least of these" (Matthew 25:40). In doing so we are doing it for Jesus himself. Whether the "least of these" came to America on slave ships from Africa, on rafts from Cuba, or smuggled in the back of a tractor trailer, I must have a heart to serve them personally and systemically. This is a way for me to practically leverage my access to resources and my personal privilege as an insider in order to honor those who are in lack.

SPEECH

When I speak in ways to lift up others who are beaten down by life and circumstances, even for those whose own choices placed them in the situation in which they find themselves, I honor them. Refusing to put people down who are already down-and-out is an honorable practice.

As a radio talk show host in Washington, DC, I see and hear a lot of dishonoring communication in the name of Christianity. It breaks my heart to hear dishonoring speech that rips apart individuals and demonizes people in order to build up someone's political or spiritual view. I believe that good, honest, and healthy debate is a great way to learn and challenge thinking; I'm all for debate. But when heated debate and disagreement turn into personal attacks, the demoralizing of opponents, character assassination, and mean-spiritedness, I must draw the line. Even in disagreement our faith must guide us toward a no-tolerance policy for mean-spiritedness. I have witnessed mean-spirited speech on Christian radio shows when the host, callers, and guests were debating politics, legalities, and even Scripture passages (which I find ironic). If the basis for our debate is the Bible, then we are surely aware that God's Word never justifies mean-spirited or divisive speech.

One of the practical ways we as believers can honor others is through speech that is bridled and beneficial for the listener. We honor God and people by refraining from telling racial jokes that injure and verbal digs that degrade. When someone says something negative about a particular people group, we can open our mouths and offer an opposing example that is positive.

I remember a man at a workshop stating how terrible Koreans were. He was an African American man in his fifties and he loathed the fact that Koreans were, as he put it, taking all the money from his community through their business practices. He referred to the Korean-owned grocery stores, liquor stores, and cleaners in his community and said he resented them. He finished his tirade by saying, "I don't know one good Korean. Do you?"

I responded by asking him many questions publicly in this gathering of about forty people. I then told him that I knew many good Korean people, those who owned shops and those who didn't.

He pressed me publicly and said aloud, "Sure, Reverend, whatever you say. I bet you don't even know one good Korean. If so, then go ahead, name one. I'd like to meet him."

I retorted, "Then I would like to invite you to my home for dinner because my wife is Korean and she's lovely!"

After he picked up his jaw from the floor, he realized how callous his words were and fell back in his chair. The participants in the class laughed and cried. None of us will forget that workshop. The issue with this man wasn't the point he was making about Korean businesses but the lumping together of Koreans in a pejorative manner. Debating the matters related to businesses in the inner city is a discussion worth having, but the grouping of a nationality with negative descriptors and generalized language is inappropriate.

In such a racially tense world you will have many opportunities to balance callous words and dishonoring speech with opposing personal examples that are honoring and positive. Please take advantage of these opportunities.

SOCIAL MEDIA

How does dishonoring someone through social media look different from dishonoring someone in person? Are people bolder online to say things that they would never say face-to-face? When challenging topics come up, do you see comment sections filled with language and responses that communicate honor, dignity, and respect, or are you more likely to see hate, venom, and antagonism? If you're anything like me, you have a love-hate relationship with social media these days. A person can get overwhelmed as they see its potential for mobilizing people toward social change, while also seeing the kind of harm and hatred it can perpetuate.

I believe the potential for unhealthy interactions online can escalate during times of increased focus on issues of injustice. When movements of digital activism rise up, sometimes it feels like divides get deeper and polarization gets stronger. It's not uncommon for us to bring strong emotions tied to deep pain when expressing our passion to shed light on ignored issues, convince our counterparts, and incite change. When we post and comment from this place of passion we can be so consumed with being heard that the value of honoring those on the other side of the screen is pushed down the priority list. Oftentimes we use social media like a megaphone, and megaphones are not a two-way communication device. Megaphones are meant to blast your message to anyone within earshot. They don't communicate nuance and are not described as graceful. I don't know about you, but I can't think of a time when my mind has been changed by someone shouting at me through a megaphone. When we are in our megaphone mode, rarely do we listen to discover the other person's deeper fears and needs. Rarely do we approach disagreements, especially ones where we believe the other person has harmful views, by building a bridge first and then leading them to our side. Instead at some point, we are convinced that the pathway to address these issues online is to dishonor and degrade. We consider it a win when we drop the mic and walk away.

Digital gracism has the value of honoring those on the other side of the screen ingrained in its approach. As you stand tall as a truth-teller bringing light to injustice, as you look to convince your counterparts to change their minds, as you hold accountable those with harmful views, you do so not with a one-sided megaphone. Instead, you do so with a listening ear and words that do not tear down, but build up. If we truly care about the parts of our body that we disagree with, we prioritize engagement over entrapment. As we lift our voices to advocate for change, instead of matching the hostility of those that disagree with us, we'll match the love and wisdom of our Savior. We have to be savvy in this era of misinformation and algorithms that are meant to prey on our weaknesses. Just because something you see online supports your side of an argument does not mean it is true or worth reposting. There are actually a lot of unseen divisive, distrustful, and divergent voices online that are strategically looking to lead people astray. Let's commit to have our bridge-building voices stand out in the chaos of polarized, politicized, and radicalized hate. With our online voice let us not merely condemn injustice but work for justice that builds toward peace.

Practically, let me give you five dos and five don'ts for being an online bridge builder and a digital gracist.

Practice these skills:

1. Ask good questions

2. Speak to the deeper fears and pain of your counterparts

3. Speak the truth and do so in love

4. Check facts before you repost

5. Let social media be an onramp to face-to-face interactions

Avoid these actions:

1. Using comment sections to name call

2. Only posting as a megaphone for your party-line politics

3. Posting sarcastic memes that belittle

4. Ruining your reputation because you posted before you prayed

5. Forgetting to unplug and go offline regularly

STEWARDSHIP

We are all given positions and resources to steward for giving honor to others. Here's an example of how I've seen this lived out. A short time ago I was able to gather a number of people in my network together to hear about an opportunity to financially support the work of Gracism Global, the organization that I lead which is growing to advance the work of racial healing around the world. This was a room full of generous friends of mine who were eager to hear about and consider donating their finances to see new bridges built across racially divisive lines. I get a special joy in introducing like-hearted friends to each other, and on this particular evening I got to do just that. You have to understand that I was floored when what I thought was going to be a new introduction between two of my friends turned out to be a reunion for two people that I didn't know had an unbelievable history with one another.

One friend was recently released from prison. After thirty-eight years of being incarcerated for a crime he did not commit, an organization called The Innocence Project helped build a case to exonerate him from the original conviction which was delivered to him as a teenager. He, a black male, along with two other friends, was convicted of murder due to the testimony of a white police officer. He spent his adult life unjustly paying the punishment for something he was innocent of. Now he is building his life as a free man and finding a unique platform of purpose addressing racial inequality in the justice system.

The other friend is an African man from Nigeria who moved to the states and built his life and family here in the suburbs of Maryland. As long as I have known him, he has been a successful entrepreneur and businessman. I knew a little bit about his career before he began his entrepreneurial ventures, but that night I found out more about his time serving as a prison guard. I discovered that evening that he was not just any prison guard, but a prison guard at the very institution where my other friend had been locked up.

When they saw each other at this event, you can imagine their shock as they recognized one another. They began to tell me this story of their connection years ago. My formerly incarcerated friend went on to share that out of all the prison guards he had interacted with over his thirty-eight years, this man he stood with that night was one of only a few that treated him with dignity, value, and honor.

My African brother stewarded his position as a correctional officer to give special honor to those the world had wanted to forget about. As he reflected on his memories of my friend who had been imprisoned, he said, "I always knew there was something different about him. By the way he carried himself and the way he treated me, I knew he didn't belong there." Both men left a lasting impression on one another because of the way they honored each other even as they stood on opposite sides of the bars of the cell.

There we stood, three black men about the same age, who had lived drastically different lives and had been awarded drastically different advantages, privileges, and social honor. But the power of gracism tied us together. Each of us lived lives where we stewarded our positions, our resources, and our relationships for the purpose of giving special honor to those who are different from ourselves.

SITTING

When is the last time you sat with someone who lacked honor? Think of a patient in the hospital, someone in rehab for an addiction, or someone who's out of work. Think of someone who is homebound, someone who moves slowly, or an elderly person who simply wants to tell stories. In our fast-paced world, the ministry of sitting with people may be the most powerful ministry of all.

By assigning greater-than value to the marginalized, the playing field of honor is leveled, God is pleased, and everyone feels better. I spend a good amount of time sitting with people who I like and who are like me in meetings, in cars, on planes, at meals, and in living room recliners. I mention this because I've become aware that there was a season in my life when I shielded myself from sitting with elderly people in need of conversation or visitation; I went way too long without visiting anyone in the hospital psych ward or prisoners. In realizing this I have become more proactive to exercise through the discipline of sitting. I have worked out by sitting on park benches with the homeless, by making more hospital visits myself instead of sending someone else. I still have the calling to minister to those on the margins, even if it doesn't fit neatly into my gift mix or personality preferences.

Isolation from a hurting world can be addictive. The intentionality of sitting is a discipline and a privilege. In the latest season of my life I have visited with the elderly, sat with my teenage little brother, traveled to funerals to be with the grieving, given to the homeless, listened to the depressed and those experiencing mental breakdowns, called the lonely, and extended kindness to those in need in some private ways. I share this not because I feel adequate in this area. Not by far. But I also know something about myself: if I am not intentional about reaching out to those who lack, I will slip into my private world of wealth, privilege, and platform ministry in front of the masses. If I'm not careful, I can lose myself in the suburbs of my Christian faith and miss the "least of these." Jesus was intentional about not missing them, about not missing you and me.

Greater honor is given to those who lack it, according to God's Word. Therefore I must also assign greater honor to those who lack it within the body of Christ and beyond.

8

Saying Five:
I WILL STAND WITH YOU

*God has put the body together, giving greater
honor to the parts that lacked it, so that there
should be no division in the body, but that its parts
should have equal concern for each other.*

1 CORINTHIANS 12:24-25 (EMPHASIS ADDED)

There are six things that God hates, according to Proverbs, and seven that are detestable to him. "A person who stirs up conflict in the community" is the last item that elevates Solomon's list from six to seven (Proverbs 6:16-19). Throughout the Scriptures we find the same to be true. Division among believers is not of God. God hates division.

Whether in marriages, friendships, church ministries, denominations, ethnic groups, genders, or families, what is it about division that assaults the very purpose and substance of God's desire for his people?

In the Garden of Eden, division crept into the relationship between humankind and God because of the choice that Adam and Eve made to disobey God. The result was cataclysmic. The free will of humans—mixed with the temptation of the CEO of division himself, Satan—drove a wedge of separation between the Creator and his creation. The gospel message is that God so loved his created ones that he provided a way for the division to be mended through his Son, Jesus Christ, the CEO of unity.

God is one (Deuteronomy 6:4; John 10:30; 14:11; 17:22); he is totally unified in his triune divinity. God the Father, God the Son, and God the Holy Spirit are three persons in perfect unity. If God is one in his nature and we are called to be one with him, then division and unity cannot be allowed to coexist among us. John put it like this: "Whoever claims to love God yet hates a brother or sister is a liar. For whoever does not love their brother and sister, whom they have seen, cannot love God, whom they have not seen. And he has given us this command: Anyone who loves God must also love their brother and sister" (1 John 4:20-21). In other words, because God is unified in his nature, he demands that those who follow him must reflect this unity in the body of Christ. Just as the human brain commands the rest of the human body, so Jesus Christ is the head of the spiritual body, the church, and commands the body to fall in line.

Therefore, when we cling to division, we align ourselves with the kingdom of darkness, led by Satan, the ultimate divider. Unity, on the other hand, aligns us with the God of unity and with Christ, the head of the church.

When community among believers is working right, there is nothing else as beautiful, nothing else as pleasant or divine. "How good and pleasant it is / when God's people live together in unity," declares the psalmist (Psalm 133:1).

MIGHTY PRAYERS

Praying together unifies people at the deepest level more than does any other spiritual practice I know. Praising God together is a close second. Prayer, however, brings us to our most humble place of dependence together.

The model prayer. Jesus taught a model prayer for his disciples to follow (Matthew 6:9-13). The first phrase of the prayer, "Our Father," identifies the commonality of our spiritual and familial relationship to God. We are part of one family as brothers and sisters in Christ. When brothers and sisters dwell together in unity, it honors God and blesses people.

While some measure of sibling rivalry is normal in families, as a dad my heart is broken whenever my children fight with each other. I want the family to be in unity and to not be at odds with each other. Disagreements are okay, but when discussion turns into words of anger and hate, I am dismayed and begin the discipline process if agreement and forgiveness don't soon transpire. I can only imagine what our heavenly Father must feel when his children are at odds with one another. When we reaffirm in prayer that we are, indeed, children of our heavenly Father, this reminds us of our spiritual connection and responsibilities as family members.

The Master's prayer. The longest prayer of Jesus recorded in Scripture is for the oneness of believers (John 17). God hates it when the disobedience of his children creates barriers and chasms between his children. God's people have been known to make subtle choices of favoritism, exclusion, and internal hostility that break down the strength of his family bonds. These choices grow and compound to create patterns of injustice, layers of inequity, and near irreconcilable relationships that span generations. God's family is left with brokenness even though he has always called for wholeness. This is why Jesus prayed that his disciples would be one as he and the Father are one. Jesus interceded with this prayer on behalf of his disciples and all those who would come to faith through their message, which includes all of us in the twenty-first century. When I write "all of us," this means Christians throughout the entire world in this century regardless of region or affiliation. Arab Christians are just as much our Christian family members as Canadian or American, Pakistani or Indian Christians. Oneness is never achieved through a kumbaya moment that dismisses past harm, but is a miraculous commitment to confront painful elements of our relationships and pursue Christ's direction to build new bonds of trust and partnership.

The martyr's prayer. Jesus' time in the Garden of Gethsemane before his death was emotional and spiritual. After sharing with the Father his desire not to be crucified, Jesus came to a deep resolve in his heart and mind. He said to God the Father, "Yet not as I will, but as you will" (Matthew 26:39). Though Jesus may have been divided in his emotions, he submitted his will to the Father's will for the purpose of regaining oneness among humankind and God, reversing the effects of division born in the Garden of Eden.

Going back to the model prayer, it begins with "Our Father" and continues to focus on God's purpose in the first half of the prayer. Indeed the prayer can easily be viewed in halves. The first half is a prayer to the Father about himself and his purposes (Matthew 6:9-10). The second half of the prayer is addressed to the Father about us as humans and our needs (vv. 11-13). Below I have quoted the first half of the prayer. Pay special attention to how Jesus ended this half.

> Our Father in heaven,
> hallowed be your name,
> your kingdom come,
> your will be done,
>   on earth as it is in heaven. (Matthew 6:9-10)

Did you see the connection? Jesus taught in his model prayer that we are to pray for God's will to be done, just as he would later do in the Garden of Gethsemane. This begs a question about God's will. While we all have our own volition, as seen in the first garden where humans originally sinned leading to separation from God, Jesus taught and modeled for us submission to the will of God. In both prayers, the model and martyr's prayers, Jesus demonstrated the priority of God's will on earth. The model prayer doesn't simply pray for God's will but specifies what that will is and where it is to happen, namely "on earth as it is in heaven."

MULTICULTURAL PRAISE

In order for us to know what God's will on earth is "as it is in heaven," we must get a picture of heaven. Allow the passage below to paint the picture better than my words could. The believers in heaven sing a new song:

> You are worthy to take the scroll
>   and to open its seals,
> because you were slain,
>   and with your blood you purchased for God
>   persons from every tribe and language and people
>   and nation.
> You have made them to be a kingdom and priests to
>   serve our God,
>   and they will reign on the earth. (Revelation 5:9-10)

In a loud voice they sing:

> Worthy is the Lamb, who was slain,
>   to receive power and wealth and wisdom
>   and strength
>   and honor and glory and praise! (Revelation 5:12)

And together multitudes worship:

> After this I looked and there before me was a great multitude that no one could count, from every nation, tribe, people and language, standing before the throne and before the Lamb. (Revelation 7:9)

Jesus is the Lamb of God who was slain by humans whom he purchased with his blood. The population of the redeemed in heaven are racially, ethnically, and nationally diverse. How beautiful! Do you see why Jesus' model prayer and martyr's prayer are connected regarding God's will? The will of God is that all of the redeemed would be one on earth as it is, and will be, in heaven.

Does your will conform to the will of God? We can choose division, as was true of the first Adam in the first garden, or submission, as was true of the second Adam in the second garden (Romans 5:12-17). God's will is that we, as his children, are unified in love and worship on earth as in heaven.

The model and martyr's prayers were bridged by the Master's prayer for unity in John 17. Jesus prayed that the unity of believers would be complete so that the world would know the love of God by witnessing it. He pleaded that they "be brought to complete unity. Then the world will know that you sent me and have loved them even as you have loved me" (John 17:23). What a mighty connection among the three prayers of Jesus!

Division on any basis is not an option for Jesus' church. If Jesus was concerned about it and had to pray for it, how much more should we pray for it? God's desire is for his church to be a "house of prayer for *all* nations" (Isaiah 56:7, emphasis added).

STANDING TOGETHER

The diversities of giftedness, gender, race, class, perspectives, and preferences may collide and even compete at times.

Grace within relationships then becomes the oil that keeps the body working together toward the goal of unity while fending off division within the body of Christ.

It is in this vein that the next saying—"I will stand with you"—emerges. In 1 Corinthians 12:24, Paul said, "God has put the body together, giving greater honor to the parts that lacked it," as we discussed in chapter seven. Notice the verse that follows: "so that there should be no division in the body." Did you catch it? When we don't assign greater honor to those who lack it, the door of division is thrown wide open.

Those who lack honor may over time become resentful, angry, or even bitter if they feel continually walked on, overlooked, underappreciated, underpaid, or discriminated against. If the undervalued are not given honor, they may rise up to fight for honor. This may come through in what they post on social media, their attitudes toward those on the other side, engaging in political action, participating in peaceful protests, or even lashing out in violent acts of retaliation. The giving or withholding of honor has enormous implications for the widening of division in our world.

Can you see these words of Scripture being played out on our national landscape? As people in the black community experience the dishonoring and dehumanizing effects of racism, we have seen, in recent years, more and more public expressions of pain, anger, and a determination to inspire change. One way to understand the protests and uprisings that have emerged in response to the loss of black life at the hands of police officers is to look at how dishonor might be at the root of this division. When life itself is dishonored, the grief that rushes in can only be constrained to an extent before it overflows. I know it is difficult for some of my white brothers and sisters to understand the mass expressions of pain and anger that are embedded within these protests, but I implore you to consider that this might be what unconstrained grief looks like.

I will never forget the conversation I had with former congressman, pastor, and civil rights leader the Reverend Walter Fauntroy. He explained to me, when discussing his role in the life of Dr. Martin Luther King Jr. as a social activist and civil rights organizer, how those who are disenfranchised and discriminated against begin to feel embittered toward the powers that be. The pain of their powerlessness and invisibility mounts up into volcanic anger toward those who live safe and secure lives. If it is perceived that the haves are the cause of some people being have-nots, then the have-nots become embittered toward the haves. More crassly put, Fauntroy said that if those who *have* don't share with those who *don't*, then it will only be a matter of time before those who *don't have* will try to violently take it. When the have-nots believe that the thing being held back from them is justice itself, the haves must not ignore the peaceful protests, marches, and calls for change only to wait until the division widens and the point of frustration rises to its boiling point.

Paul addresses the dilemma of division that could potentially cause a breach within the body. He offers an answer that will prevent division, namely giving greater honor to those who are deficient of it. Don't ignore them; exalt them. Honor them. Help them. Lift them up. Use your power to encourage, inspire, protect, and bring them into the fold. In so doing you will fend off the thing that God hates—division. Racism, discrimination, segregation, and classism divide, but gracism unites. Gracism heals.

So the next time you check the news and see of another protest, march, or uprising and you think to yourself how divided this world has become, let your next thought be one that moves you to seek to comprehend the pain that a person or community must feel to cry out in such a way. I am simply encouraging a heart attitude that seeks to bless first and judge second.

SAVE THE RHINOS

The television news show 60 *Minutes*, with Dan Rather, reported on white rhinos in South Africa. Though the white rhino population is a protected species, the news story reported that they were being killed off one by one. There was a season when 10 percent of the white rhino population was being hunted. Game park rangers were unsure of what was happening since there was no evidence from the dead rhino carcasses of poachers or hunters. After investigation, a shocking discovery was made. As hard as it was to believe, rangers discovered that teenage elephants were killing the rhinos. It was very unusual for elephants to be predators. Rangers began to tag the elephants and document their behavior through surveillance. Like having a criminal rap sheet on each of the elephants, it was documented that a group of adolescent elephants were the culprits. Why would teenage elephants become predatory bullies acting as juvenile delinquents? The answer went back fifteen to twenty years. Because of the overpopulation of elephants in South Africa, much like deer in my part of the country, there was an official choice made to kill the adult elephants and relocate the baby elephants by airlifting them to another part of the country. After a decade of growing up in the wild without the adult elephants as an influence, the younger elephants had no guidance as to what was right and wrong. The younger elephants grew up without anyone teaching them that killing rhinos was inappropriate behavior for elephants.

Seeking a solution that would not involve killing the delin-
quent elephants, the rangers made a corrective decision they
hoped would solve the problem. The officials airlifted a group
of adult elephants to the wildlife area where the younger delinquents lived. Within a short period of time, the older elephants reestablished order and authority. The killing ended.
What an amazing documentary! When I watched it, I was
moved because I realized that God has established order even
within the animal kingdom. In addition, the story speaks to so
many of our social issues—mentoring, crime, security, authority, community, and even the role of the elderly in our
multigenerational society. Because the delinquents had no
role models, they ran rampant and brought disorder to the
environment, harming the preserved species.

Had there been no one to stand for the white rhinos, maybe
they would be extinct in South Africa now. Figuratively
speaking, who is standing up for the white rhinos in your
family or neighborhood? Who is standing for the rhinos in our
country, in our cities, or in our congregations? Maybe you feel
like a white rhino who is in an unsafe environment and you
feel helpless. You deeply desire for someone with the resources to stand with you, to stand up for you. Whoever the
white rhinos are in any given sociological environment, they
need protection from harmful elephants. Whether the harm
is intentional or unintentional, natural or unnatural, inter-
vention is necessary to solve the problem.

Imagine how the heart of God is warmed when his children
get along in peace. Elephants and rhinos living together in
safety is better than killing and death, right? Once safety and
value are established, then community and communion have
a chance. Imagine what heaven must feel when all of God's
children in Christ dwell together in unity.

What a wonderful answer to Jesus' prayer when you and I put aside our differences and choose to stand together! Moreover what a unifying goal when you and I stand together to give greater honor to those in our community who are lacking it! It unifies us when we have a common goal to elevate, protect, and preserve the lowly among us, whoever they are—whether rhinos, young or old elephants, or officials making choices that affect the entire society.

GRACISM AT THE UKRAINE BORDER

Early in 2022 I was asked to give a short word and lead a prayer for a meeting involving believers in leadership from around the world. Shortly after that prayer call, I received an email from Ivan, a brother in Christ who had heard me speak that day. He said he was from Ukraine and asked me to pray specifically for him and his ministry. Please know that at this point in history the conflict in Ukraine hadn't yet broken out and rumors of Russia's amassing troops at the border were just starting to be mentioned in the news. Since I knew little of Ukraine and had no previous ministry interest in that region, I can only credit my response to this young pastor to the Spirit's urging. Over the next month we would pray together on a few occasions. When I finally had serious fear that conflict might soon become a reality in that area and asked him about it, he would say, "The only two countries who are not worried that there will be war between Russia and Ukraine are Russia and Ukraine." He reassured me that Putin had flexed his military muscles like this before and would soon fall back. So you can imagine both of our surprise when on February 24, Russia launched a full-scale invasion and my friend Ivan had to immediately pack up his family to flee for the border, and he himself became a refugee.

Ivan and I would video chat as he was on the run and he would give me updates of his strategic work to serve his brothers and sisters in Christ in escaping the war-torn areas as well. Our church was able to send money for supplies and fuel for those making the dangerous journey fleeing their homeland. Days later, on one of our calls, Ivan asked me to pray about bringing over a team of bridge builders to minister to and serve those refugees coming out of Ukraine.

Here was an invitation to not just stand with our brother in word and in spirit, but to actually cross the ocean and stand with him and his fellow refugees in the flesh. He made it clear that he could not promise our safety, but he could promise that there were people and needs for which the Lord could use us. After serious deliberation with the Lord, my elders, advisers, and most importantly my wife, I agreed to lead this delegation and travel to Ukraine. We arrived at the Ukraine border just one month after the initial invasion and spent ten days traveling with my friend Ivan and his associates to meet with, cry with, encourage, bless, and hand-deliver supplies into Ukraine during their time of need. They told us stories of pain and trauma. The women told us the names of their husbands, brothers, and fathers who had to stay and fight. They showed us pictures of their homes they had to leave behind. A common theme in each of our conversations was that they were very much alone and life at that moment was filled with many fearful unknowns.

Joining Ivan in this work by not just praying for him or sending money to him, but physically standing with him in those moments of ministry to his fellow refugees, meant something valuable to him. We brought the prayers of care, financial resources, and strategic connections of our support system from back home. But in those moments, the value came in the physical presence of someone to stand with them in their time of need.

Have you ever had an experience like that where you have expressed moral support for a brother or sister as they faced some intense challenges, and then there was an opportunity to take a risk, make a sacrifice, and stand with them? Have you ever shown up for that court hearing, walked beside them at a protest, made a statement at the school board meeting, sat beside them as they approached HR, stood with them as they faced the bully, or spoken up for them when your family member said something racist?

Those in Ukraine were facing the challenges of oppression, need, and fear that come with the extreme case of the conflict which became the largest ground war in Europe since WWII. But, here in the United States, many of our own closer brothers and sisters speak of challenges of oppression, need, and fear associated with the racial harm that continues to be woven throughout the stories of this country's ethnic minority groups. Instead of just offering your moral support and a promise of prayer, your physical presence and active partnership in pushing back against the challenges that affect them most will be what truly communicates your commitment to oneness with them.

HOW DO I SIGN UP FOR THIS?

Practically speaking, how can we live out the "I will stand with you" saying? When you and I agree to stand with and for the disenfranchised, we are being gracists. We are standing in the gap for those who may not be able to speak for themselves. And many times, even when they do speak, their voices are silenced, ignored, or suppressed. You and I have friends and networks, political connections, board contacts, and sometimes simply a hand of invitation to the table of feasting that can be a gesture of standing with someone on the fringes.

Standing with people sometimes means standing up for people. My goal in this book has been to press the principles of gracism into our hearts and minds with the hopes that God will show you and me practical ways to apply these principles when the opportunity presents itself in our context. I believe that God always gives us opportunities to apply what we learn. My prayer is that God will show you your open door of opportunity to be a gracist in some way today or this week.

There are times when much more may be required of a gracist. In times of overt discrimination, or covert racism and injustice, it may be required of you and me to stand up for the rights of those whose voices have been muted by the powers that be. You may find yourself in the halls of Congress speaking up for those who have been silenced, on the streets of your city marching for a cause, in the ballot booth of your local school voting for a candidate who will serve the disenfranchised, or simply in the choir director's office speaking for a choir member in the church who is not getting an opportunity to sing like others; the principle is the same. Stand up for the needy. Speak up for the silenced. Rise up for those whose wings are clipped. Stand!

STANDING BY GRACE

Jesus quoted from the prophet Isaiah when he publicly read,

> The Spirit of the Lord is on me,
>   because he has anointed me
>   to proclaim good news to the poor.
> He has sent me to proclaim freedom for the prisoners
>   and recovery of sight for the blind,

to set the oppressed free,
    to proclaim the year of the Lord's favor.
    (Luke 4:18-19)

After closing the scroll from which he read in the synagogue, Jesus exclaimed, "Today this scripture is fulfilled in your hearing" (Luke 4:21).

This must have freaked out the religious leaders of the day, who were used to smug piety and clerical segregation from the commoners. Jesus was a gracist. He reached out to the poor and the prisoners, the disabled and the oppressed, so that they would not be divided from him or us. You and I can stand only because of his grace. None of us would have a thing were it not for the grace of God in our lives. If God were not a gracist, you and I would have no power, no pleasure, no purpose, and no possessions. If you have the ability to read, hear, or understand this sentence, you have been graced. Therefore for any of us to ever feel justified in being elitist, arrogant, or cocky in any way would be absurd, wouldn't it?

If not for grace, we would still be marginalized on the fringes of salvation awaiting eternal judgment. There is no room for boasting about gifts, talents, capabilities, abilities, heritage, race, or ethnicity. Paul knew firsthand of such temptation. When evaluating his religiosity through circumcision, nationalism through Israel, tribalism through Benjamin, ethnocentrism as a Hebrew of Hebrews, and elitism through Pharisaical status, Paul counted it all as garbage compared to gaining salvation through Jesus Christ and the surpassing greatness of knowing him intimately (Philippians 3:5-9).

When Paul wrote the striking fact "It is by grace you have been saved, through faith—and this is not from yourselves, it is the gift of God—not by works, so that no one can boast" (Ephesians 2:8-9), he was talking about himself, the early

Christians, and us. The propensity to forget that we are saved and sustained by grace (God's ridiculous favor) is overwhelmingly natural. To be reminded of the grace it took to save us is exactly the pride adjustment I need whenever I get too big for my britches.

The special grace of God keeps us levelheaded and reminds us that we are all one in Christ. We are all redeemed by grace regardless of our distinctions. How ridiculous it would be to separate over these very distinctions! Therefore, since Christ stood in the gap for you and me, will you now have that same attitude to stand with and for others? Not as their savior, but because of the Savior. If we will do this, the forces of division will be thwarted among believers. Will you say to others on the fringes, "I will stand with you when you are mistreated, devalued, ignored, or left out"? I believe that when choruses of believers sing this phrase *I will stand with you* with passion and conviction for one another, true unity will abound. Otherwise the result will be the dissension and division God hates.

9

Saying Six:
I WILL CONSIDER YOU

*God has put the body together, giving greater
honor to the parts that lacked it, so that there
should be no division in the body, but that its parts
should have equal concern for each other.*

1 CORINTHIANS 12:24-25 (EMPHASIS ADDED)

Have you ever driven through a major city and come to a stoplight where there was a person dressed in ragged clothes limping toward your car seeking a handout? Or maybe you have taken a walk down an urban street or visited a tourist area only to be confronted by someone who gave you a sad story of his need for money to catch a bus or get something to eat. How does it make you feel when that happens to you?

Would anyone reading this book be honest enough to confess that there are times when you have wanted to cross the street before the panhandler approached you? Have you ever hoped that the light would turn green before the moment of decision faced you, easing your conscience?

This has happened to me on multiple occasions. It is never easy to watch someone who is poor or downtrodden struggle. Being on the frontline of poverty is disconcerting, to say the least. Moreover it is tempting to be judgmental about the motives of the person asking for money. We surmise that she will use it to buy drugs or alcohol. We excuse our inaction with our busy schedules, not having time to stop and give money, food, or even a look of dignity to someone we carelessly label as a "bum."

THE OTHER SIDE

What would Jesus do in this kind of situation? He explained it in his own words in Luke 10:30-37. Jesus told the story of a man who was lying on the side of the road, having been beaten by robbers and left for dead. A priest witnessed the man's downtrodden state and yet crossed the road and walked down the other side of the street without helping him. After the priest got as far from the helpless man as possible, a Levite (another kind of religious leader of the day) also passed by the man who had been mugged. Like the priest, the Levite passed by on the other side of the road to avoid contact with the man, absolving himself of responsibility and leaving the victim for someone else to help.

Finally, a third man encountered the downtrodden soul lying on the ground. This man was a Samaritan, one who was racially mixed with Jewish blood. The Samaritan took pity on the man. His concern for the hurt man drove him to action. He bandaged the victim's wounds, pouring oil and wine on him. He then picked up the man and placed him on his donkey, escorting him to a local inn, where he invested his own resources to assure that the victim's stay was paid for.

THREE LOVING ACTS OF GRACE

The Samaritan did three loving things that underscored the point about loving one's neighbor that Jesus was teaching through this parable. First, the Samaritan "took pity" on the downtrodden man (Luke 10:33). This means he had a *merciful heart*. Second, the Samaritan took action by bandaging the man's wounds and escorting him to a safe place where he could heal. This demonstrates a *shepherding heart*. The third act of love by the Samaritan was to invest in the healing of the victim by paying the innkeeper for the time spent in the inn, offering additional money if the man needed to stay longer. The Samaritan showed a *generous heart* as he gave of his finances.

When we see the condition of the Samaritan's heart, we aren't looking for spiritual gifts of mercy, shepherding, and giving. We are seeing a transformed heart that beats the way Jesus' heart would beat; beyond. Giftedness is graciousness. It's a heart thing.

In a polarized society like ours we regularly encounter people who represent the other side of issues about which we have strong convictions. What are we to do when we see "those people" hurting? Jesus taught us to love them with active compassion. The heart attitudes of the first two characters focused only on how to avoid the problem, while the third character engaged the problem as an opportunity to love. A concerned heart should lead to compassionate actions. What is our heart like? Is it a heart that seeks to avoid those in need or one that engages the problem as an opportunity to love? Is it a heart that only is concerned with the dignity of those that are on our side or will we cross the road to show mercy to those that hold beliefs that make our lives harder?

Unfortunately the religious leaders were more focused on their beliefs than on living out their faith through loving actions. This is the heart of eternal life. Jesus said, "Do this and you will live" (Luke 10:28). Eternal life is found in God's love for us and our love for God. It is a relationship of love and response. Such vibrancy in a true relationship of intimacy with God will overflow into our human relationships and acts of compassion. How could it not? When we have been touched by God's compassion and mercy, it would be scandalous to not be compassionate and merciful to others. A heart that is eternally alive beats with the rhythms of mercy, shepherding care, and generosity; even toward the "other."

The priest and the Levite were too concerned about themselves, their schedules, status, and other preoccupations, to see the point that Jesus was making in the parable, namely that love and compassion take action. The recipients of the action are those in need, those who are hurting or downtrodden, and those who represent the other end of a divided, polarized society.

How are you doing with such gracist acts of outreach in our world of seemingly greater isolation and guardedness from those who are on the outside of your comfortable in-group? Isn't it curious to you that these are exactly the ones with whom Jesus hung out? He was always mixing it up with sinners, tax collectors, prostitutes, the blind, the hungry, and those from different ethnic backgrounds than his own. What is that all about? Jesus had a merciful, concerned, bridge-building heart; what about us?

GETTING BACK ON THE RIGHT SIDE OF THE STREET

Even as I am writing this page I am feeling the conviction of God's Spirit. I confess to you that I'm not gracist enough. I seek isolation and protection from the ills of society, which includes the people who go with those ills. These are the people whom Christ was seeking to hang out with and touch. Yet in my world of cul-de-sac living, garage door closing, back deck relaxing, and mountaintop retreating, I can easily shut out the undesirable people whose pain is too much for me to bear. Would you pause with me for a prayer of confession and forgiveness?

Dear Lord, please forgive me for my insensitivities toward the hurting and downtrodden. Please forgive me for acting like the priest and Levite more often than the Samaritan. Help me to be more gracist in my life, more concerned. Father, I thank you for your grace, mercy, and compassion on me. Thank you for not leaving me on the side of the road. Help me to extend that kind of love to more people in my world. I pray in Jesus' name; Amen.

I WILL CONSIDER YOU

How can we have "equal concern" like Paul spoke of in 1 Corinthians 12:24-25? Do you remember what he said? "God has put the body together, giving greater honor to the parts that lacked it, so that there should be no division in the body, but that its parts should have equal concern for each other."

Self-preoccupation can keep Christians from experiencing the multicultural, multiracial, and multidenominational unity God desires for us. When Christians stop reacting negatively to sociopolitical terminology like *affirmative action, special interest,* or *equal opportunity,* and instead use Paul's terms *special honor, greater honor,* and *equal concern,* it will change our attitudes from a "me and mine" to a "we and ours" mentality. Instead of holding on to the attitudes of the priest and Levite, let's cling to the Samaritan's merciful heart. Jesus said, "Go and do likewise" (Luke 10:37).

The sixth saying of a gracist is "I will consider you." I will concern myself with your feelings and your dreams whether

I'm walking down the street like the good Samaritan or in the halls of Congress voting for the things that concern you. I will make it my concern to hear your experience and seek to understand your fears. I will not develop my opinions about matters that concern you without doing the deeply meaningful work of listening to your perspective and considering what is most important to you.

EQUAL CONCERN

The term Paul used for equal concern literally means "same care" and has the idea of possessing an anxious interest at the same level that I would have for myself or one I love.

Equal concern invites the question, equal to whom? Paul said that we should have equal concern for each other. I should be thinking about your interest and you should be thinking about mine. This means that I am to consider your thoughts, perspectives, and feelings rather than making a unilateral decision that might adversely affect you. There is not one group that should be ignored or passed over. All should be included if possible and considered always. Gracists consider the concerns of others who are not like them, those of a different giftedness, color, gender, educational, or class category. Would there not be less church division if people were bent on radical inclusivity and made it a normal practice to pause in consideration of other's feelings and perspectives? Boy, wouldn't marriages be happier if spouses employed the equal-concern principle of gracism with each other? Wouldn't relationships soar if gracism were rampant?

THEM AND US?

Paul was saying that there should not be a "them versus us" mentality in the body of Christ. My concern for "them" should be just as deep as my concern for "us." I was broadened in my thinking about this when I engaged in an intellectually stimulating conversation for several hours with former President Bill Clinton about race relations along with a small group of religious leaders. When asked about racial reconciliation and its importance, President Clinton told a story of growing up in Arkansas in a single-parent household where neighbors were repeatedly invited over. At that point, the people who were known as "them" became the "us" by virtue of the fact that they were in his home regularly. Houseguests were no longer "those people" across the street but they were a part of "us." We are them and they are us. Furthering the discussion he said (I am paraphrasing), "If something negative or unfortunate happened to our neighbors who lived across the street who we had over continually, it was as if it were happening to us because they were 'us.'" He said that it is natural to have a "them versus us" mentality until people are invited into your home.

I realized then, and still believe now, that the "them versus us" mentality plagues race relations, denominational distinctions, and cultural differences to such a degree that it is hard for compassion to cross over to the other side of the street. If I don't see the man lying on the side of the road as one who is a part of my family, ethnicity, religious group, or class, then it is easier to dismiss him.

It is difficult to find any prevailing issue where this polarizing "them versus us" mentality does not dominate the discussion. It seems like every time a leading issue is brought up, whether online or in person, we have come to expect overwhelming attempts of each party to bully the other side into submission. The winner is determined by who can set up the best "gotcha" comment. Each person is consumed with trying to get the other side to consider their own perspective. Taking the initiative to consider the hopes, dreams, fears, and concerns of the other side is out of the question, let alone taking compassionate action to be merciful, generous, and shepherding on top of that. To hear a pro-lifer say to a pro-choicer, "I think I'm beginning to understand where you're coming from" would about knock you off your chair. Or if an NRA lobbyist would publicly acknowledge the concerns of a school shooting victim's family, you might wonder if the video was doctored. If a protestor and a police officer actually listened to the fears of one another and considered them with equal concern, what could that do to address the division, damage, and disparity plaguing communities around the country?

Jesus so loved the world that he bridged the gap between humanity and heaven by becoming like us and empowering us to become like him. When we begin to see people of different backgrounds as "us" and not as "them," we will be able to minister compassion and mercy at deeper levels of identification. When we see the victimized man on the side of the road, we must not see him as an "other" but as a brother in our family of humanity who needs our concern.

The phrase "equal concern" (or anxious interest) from 1 Corinthians 12:25 is the same terminology Paul used in 2 Corinthians 11:28 when he said, "Besides everything else, I face daily the pressure of my concern for all the churches." Notice Paul's concern for all the churches. He had anxious interest and varying concerns about all the churches under his apostleship. It was the same kind of concern that a parent has for multiple children. I don't know of one parent who wishes for the success of one child while desiring for another child to fail. Conversely, while the path of success for each child is different, the parent's interest in the success of each child is equally fervent.

Paul was saying that we are all one; we are all connected in one body—the church—with one head of that body, Jesus Christ. Therefore we must have equal concern for one another regardless of our distinctions. There is no "them" and "us" in the body of Christ. And on a broader human scale the distinctions between unredeemed and redeemed humans are not as vastly different as we might think. We may not all be the same in our redemptive status, but we all have the potential to be since Jesus Christ died for all humans and not just for one class or race of people. Therefore I must view every person not from a worldly viewpoint but from a spiritual point of view where I see them as Jesus Christ sees them (2 Corinthians 5:16).

FERGUSON 2014

At the end of the summer in 2014 the names Michael Brown and Darren Wilson were found in every news program and front page headline around the country. Ferguson, Missouri, went from being an unknown municipality in St. Louis to being the epicenter of racial conflict in recent times. A white police officer was standing trial before a grand jury to determine whether or not he would face charges for shooting and killing a young black man while in the line of duty. The protests in the streets of Ferguson demonstrated that this tragic loss of life was the breaking point for a community that had been crushed under crippling laws and unjust enforcement. At this point, no one knew that what was happening in Ferguson would come to be the first of many uprisings around the country following further instances of black men dying at the hands of police officers.

While the city was in turmoil, a white pastor friend of mine, who leads a large church in the St. Louis area, reached out to me with a heavy heart. He was determined to do something, but he had no roadmap for how to respond in a situation like this. He told me that although he didn't know what to do, he knew he couldn't do nothing. He wanted to step in and engage with the situation, and he asked for my help to figure out how. He invited me to bring a team to come convene a dialogue session with key community leaders in order to address the pain and chaos this community was facing. With his influential network throughout the city I had him pull together a gathering of what we called the "6 P Community Influencers." Participants of this group represented police, pastors, private business owners, public educators, politicians, and protestors. This group of stakeholders had formal and informal positions of influence throughout the Ferguson and St. Louis area. Each was affected differently by the issue at hand and the tension in the room couldn't have been higher.

As the protests continued in the streets day and night, we gathered a group of about twenty-five people in the basement of the First Baptist Church of Ferguson. Among others, sitting around the table were the chief of police, the mayor of Ferguson, store owners, local school principals, pastors of neighborhood churches, as well as a group of around ten community members who had started a protest group called the Lost Voices. With a gathering like that, it would only be the Lord himself who could help them reach the point where they might consider the needs, perspective, and pain of each other's side.

We were just about to the end of two long days of dialogue when something happened in that room that I will never forget. We had worked through hours of tension-filled talks and deepening layers of engagement when I turned to those representing the Lost Voices and asked them, "If you could leave this conversation and have these police officers understand one thing, what would you want them to know?" The Lost Voices, in such genuine exhaustion, expressed the damage done by having police officers coldly patrol the neighborhoods, only talk to community members when giving out expensive citations, and harassing the residents for things that weren't even against the law. They said that this damage encapsulated the brokenness in their community.

I turned to the chief of police and asked him what he just heard. He thought for a few moments, turned to the community members, and in a genuinely concerned voice said, "So what you're saying is that I should instruct my officers, when they are out driving through the neighborhood, they need to get off the computer, put down the phone, drive slower, roll down the window, and just say hello." The audible gasp and cry of "YES!" that came from this protest group made it evident that they believed the police chief was finally listening. In that moment you could tell they believed that he was considering their needs, their lives, and their perspective.

I then turned to the officers and asked them a similar question to the one I asked of the protestors. I said, "If you could leave this conversation and have the community members understand one thing, what would you want them to know?" One officer spoke up and talked about what it was like for him to be working the frontlines of the protests. He described standing eye to eye with those holding signs, shouting to be heard, and leading the uprising. He talked about how he was in support of their rights to protest and he understands that when he wears his badge he represents the group that they are angry with. But then he got a little vulnerable. He said, "When I'm there serving in my position and you are screaming words of death and hate at me; when you are saying that you're going to find my family and hurt my kids—my badge doesn't shield me from that kind of hate. Behind the uniform I am still a person. Please realize those words are not helping your cause." He went on to tell them he would ensure that other officers would clearly mark out and protect the boundaries of their organized protests to reduce the influence of outside agitators.

Again, I turned to this group of protestors and asked them what they just heard. They spoke up and acknowledged the humanity of this officer and made commitments to respect him as a person even in the midst of their movement against police injustice. They then took it a step further and exchanged personal phone numbers with the officer and came up with a plan to communicate about future demonstrations.

I'm not saying that at the end of the two days of talks that these folks were reconciled and inviting each other over for Thanksgiving dinner. But, I am saying that the power of the moment came when each party began to listen to the other. Listen to their pain. Listen to their experiences. Listen to their hopes. And then to treat the other with equal concern with intentional consideration for the needs of the other.

A KOREAN CHURCH MOVE

While I was presenting a workshop to several pastors in California, a man asked a question about a move that his church was planning to make to the city. He wanted to know what I thought about the fact that his all-Korean church had purchased a piece of land in an area of the inner city that had a majority population of poor African Americans and Hispanics. The young pastor's concern was that his large Korean congregation was going to commute into the city on Sundays for church and then retreat to the suburbs after services. Because the services would be conducted in Korean, and many of those in the Korean community were not interested in building crosscultural relationships (according to this pastor), he wondered what effect such a move would have on those in the city. What a thoughtful question!

This is exactly what I mean when a gracist says "I will consider you" before making drastic moves and big decisions. Questions about the impact on a community, a ministry, an ethnic group, a class, a neighborhood, a corporation, or a department are all gracist questions that help us to consider the impact of our choices.

I affirmed the Korean brother who asked for my opinion about the Korean church moving into the urban community. I recommended ways he could build a bridge to the urban community through an English-speaking outreach ministry. He was receptive to and enlightened by the ideas. Other ideas, about how to minister to the community through initiatives that would serve the population at large, would aid the Korean church in building bridges with its neighbors and fulfilling the Great Commission at the same time. I was blessed by his consideration of the impact his church's move would have on the community.

CONSIDERING AFRICA

For every time I have been considerate, I can think of two times when I have failed to consider others in proper ways. I am working hard on living out the book I am writing. Just when I thought I was doing well, I received a letter from a church attender who was upset about my referring to Africa when speaking about real poverty. At first this may not seem like a big deal, but after reading her letter and seeing it from her perspective, it makes complete sense.

Dear Pastor Anderson,

Thank you for your ministry. I really enjoy attending Bridgeway and the multicultural ministry here. However, I had a very difficult time listening to your message on wealth when you referred to Africa and poverty. I was offended by you saying that you never saw real poverty until you went to Africa. You see, Africa is usually thought of, by many Americans, as one country. Africa is thought of as just one place where people are running around poor, in war, and living in horrific conditions. However, Africa is a continent with over fifty countries. These countries each have their own governments, people, and cultures. Just like the US and other countries, there are both urban and rural places in African countries.

Therefore, generalizing the whole continent is a big mistake that has several negative repercussions. The media, which is obviously very influential on people's ideas, tends to focus mainly on the poor, rural, diseased, or war-torn places. In fact, I am from an African country and have had people come to me and ask me questions like "So, are you going back to the war?" Then I have to explain to them that I will be going back home and that the country I am from in Africa is not experiencing any war. Other questions and comments I have heard are "Oh, thank God you were rescued from that place," "Did you wear clothes before you got here?" and "Had you ever seen a car?" The above depiction of Africa is very damaging to people who come to the US from African countries. Many employers and others assume that we are uneducated and not competent enough to fill various jobs or positions in society. Furthermore, no one wants to be involved economically with different African countries because of the perception that it is a backward place. It's always amazing to me how people often call different European countries by name. People will speak of going to Germany, France, and so on. But when many people go to African countries such as Kenya and Ethiopia, they often tend to say, "Over there in Africa." To generalize Africa this way is like referring to Europe or Asia as a country.

When you say that you haven't seen real poverty until you went to Africa and don't specify a particular country, it would be like someone saying, "I never saw a drug-dealing, ignorant person until I met an African American." Of course such a statement is very ignorant and gives a wrong perception of African Americans. It is damaging to the African American community as a whole.
Margaret Akinyi

I responded to Ms. Akinyi with a sincere apology letter.

Dear Ms. Margaret Akinyi:
First of all, I am so happy that you wrote me and that you are attending Bridgeway. I do hope that my comments, while they may have hurt you, do not at all reflect my heart on the matter of Africa as a continent. Your correction was much needed, and I receive it openly. Thank you so much for saying all that you said because I now know how my comments can be misconstrued.

Although I know that Africa is a continent and not a country, I did not know how some Africans might be hurt by non-Africans like me speaking generally and not specifically about the continent. I clearly see now that the perceptions and stereotypes that can come from lumping the countries and the continent together can have an adverse effect on the understanding of those who have not been to various African countries as I have.

Thank you so much for clarifying and sharing this with me. I feel honored to have learned this from you and will seek to always be clear when I am speaking about Africa in general and certain countries in particular. Please accept my apology for making this error out of ignorance as to how I might be contributing to misperceptions of those from Africa. Will you please forgive me?

Ms. Akinyi enlightened me on a specific way that I can be more considerate as to how the words I use affect her and others. When I speak about Africa, I now try to say "countries in Africa" or be even more specific about the actual country I'm referencing. In addition, whenever I speak about the poverty I witness there, I am careful to mention that I have met many educated people and wealthy people there as well, which is true. I do my best to make concerted efforts to include a fuller picture of the African continent amid so much media coverage about the need for assistance for the poorer populations within the various countries. Below is Ms. Akinyi's response to my letter.

Dear Pastor Anderson,
Thank you very much for your reply to my letter. I felt a burden lifted from my heart when I read your letter. I have no problem at all in forgiving you and I ask that you may forgive me too if there was anything in my letter that came out as being rude. I know that you had very good intentions when you delivered that sermon, and that is why I do not hold anything against you. God has blessed you with a powerful, unique ministry and I feel

blessed to be in Bridgeway. I will continue praying that God will continue to bless, encourage, and strengthen you, and the church as a whole. Thank you again for your encouraging letter.

Margaret

"I will consider you" is not only a gracist saying but it also is a reality of living. Striving to do what we say makes our words come alive. Gracist living is about taking the sayings of Paul and living them out in the context of our lives and relationships. For me, considering others also means considering the words I use and the concepts I purport when preaching as it relates to other people groups and parts of the world. As a leader, I have to resist the urge to brush off correction from someone I have offended by simply responding with "They just didn't understand what I was trying to say" or "Well, I had good intentions." Instead, I am committed to considering the needs, perspectives, and pain of those who are different from me and responding with grace, having equal concern for them personally. How about in your life? What does it mean for you to consider others in your areas of leadership, relationships, and even how you interact online?

10

Saying Seven:
I WILL CELEBRATE WITH YOU

If one part is honored, every part rejoices with it.

1 CORINTHIANS 12:26 (EMPHASIS ADDED)

At Bridgeway Community Church we try to circle around those who suffer. When a child dies or a loved one leaves, our church family is swift at rallying around the hurting and those broken by grief. We will provide meals so those who grieve don't have to cook. We will arrange funerals, send pastors, organize prayer times, show up at memorial services, and send flowers, cards, and money to help ease the pain of the brokenhearted. When it comes to the homeless and the hungry, we clothe and feed them through our community cupboard and donations. While there is always more to do, I am grateful for the merciful, caring, and generous hearts of our people. Many churches throughout the world reflect similar generosity. It is one of the greatest hallmarks of organized Christianity.

When others are hurting in the body, gracism demands that we sympathize with the pain of our brothers and sisters.

When someone is unfairly or unjustly treated, we should stand with that person since we are all a part of one body.

I believe, however, that our church can develop more in the area of rejoicing, as is true for many Christians. Not simply rejoicing over what God has done in our personal lives, but the kind of rejoicing that Paul mentions in 1 Corinthians 12:26, namely rejoicing with others over their successes. Just as you and I are to enter into the suffering and pain of others, so we are also to rejoice or celebrate with others. I believe that when people go through crisis and difficult times, if the church is not there to meet them in their time of need, they often wonder if the Lord himself is also absent in their time of need. If that is true in their time of need what does it communicate if the church is not there to meet them in their time of rejoicing?

When another racial group, ethnic group, or gender group succeeds in some area, instead of becoming jealous or resentful, I should celebrate. This should be especially true when those who are downtrodden finally elevate. Imagine an unemployed person in your small group Bible study weeping over his financial scarcity and the difficulty of finding another job. To make matters worse, this person doesn't have a degree; he quit his last job and has a pattern of not holding down employment due to some skill, attitude, and personality issues. As a group you all pray for this person and do what you can to help.

How would you respond if this same person arrived at the Bible study the next week celebrating the fact that he was just hired by a large company that has agreed to pay him an annual six-figure salary with full benefits, stock options, and an incentive program that would be a one-time payout of several hundred thousand dollars? Would you rejoice with him? Of course you would.

How about if you discovered that the position your group member was hired for was the same position that you applied for two months prior? You prayed for that position; you studied for the interview and hoped you would land the coveted opportunity. How would you respond? It's a bit more difficult to rejoice now, right?

I believe Paul's heart in 1 Corinthians 12 is that there will be many different kinds of people in the Christian community. Some will have greater gifts than others. Some will have a different background educationally, racially, or culturally. In all of this diversity we must rejoice with the successes of others, especially when it is not natural for us to rejoice in this way.

Do you think it is harder to rejoice with others or to suffer with them? Both can be difficult. Choosing to feel someone else's pain when I am not in pain can be challenging, but I think that rejoicing with others when I am desiring my own achievement can be even harder.

For example, look at the list below of rejoicing amid real circumstances of life. I am still called to rejoice with others

- when someone in the body is having a baby, even though I am barren

- when someone in the body gets a new car and I'm still walking

- when someone in the body gets a new job or house and I'm struggling to achieve both

- when someone in the body is getting married and I'm still single

- when someone in the body receives applause for an achievement that I wish I had

- when someone in the body had her child accepted into a college that my child didn't get into

Celebrating each other's successes and wins is critical to unity. Jealousy and covetousness brew the poison that brings dissension to the body.

I celebrate you when I encourage your success and acknowledge that you are doing well. I celebrate you when I call to offer congratulations or when I attend a party in your honor. Believe it or not, by celebrating others I am adding to the unity of the body and encouraging others in the body. Because rejoicing with others is not always easy, we need the Holy Spirit to help us.

When it comes to race relations, sometimes rejoicing can be even more difficult.

BLACK HISTORY MONTH CELEBRATIONS

Gracism Global is the consulting organization through which I train top level leaders on issues of multicultural leadership. In this role I have found that Black History Month, even today, continues to produce tension within some companies. They have questions as to whether an entire month should be set aside to celebrate one group's heritage. While some whites and others argue that a month is too long, there are blacks who argue that it is the shortest month of the year. In addition, a myriad of other issues flow from the debate. I usually land on the decision from a consultant's perspective that to participate in this annual celebration out of social obligation would do more harm than good. The African Americans on your staff and those that are your clients have a keen awareness of when a company acknowledges and takes part in these special celebrations in ways that feel meaningful or ways that feel mandatory. As a leader, you have the opportunity to weave celebrations like this into an entire culture and atmosphere that helps to value and commemorate the contributions of your minority staff. Celebration doesn't have to be limited to an event, it can be a way of life.

I have told organizations not to call me to give speeches in February. If the company brings me in to speak on race relations during other months of the year, that demonstrates to me that they are serious about matters of diversity beyond an annual nod. Companies that are genuine in their celebration of Black History Month view the celebration as one of many different celebrations and do not view it simply as a token program to appease African Americans. I can usually sense the difference between the two perspectives. The token perspective is evident when the February celebration is the only program the company has and the only people interested in attending a celebration event are its organizers, along with a few guilty stragglers. The companies that are genuine in their diversity awareness have many celebrations throughout the year as they consistently elevate the value of celebration. They observe other culturally significant dates throughout the year as well. Celebrations beyond traditional ones like Christmas and Independence Day include the following: Juneteenth, the celebration on June 19 to commemorate the abolition of slavery; Saint Patrick's Day; Asian American and Pacific Islander Heritage Month; Kwanzaa; Yom Kippur; Ramadan; and Dr. Martin Luther King Jr.'s birthday. I have been to companies that have committees, leadership teams, and boards that focus solely on developing and maintaining a culture of celebration and acceptance. In a multicultural country like ours it is very important to honor and rejoice with others who find significance in their upbringing and backgrounds.

For churches, cultural celebrations can be tricky because celebrating Jesus Christ is where we as Christians find our greatest joy and commonality. Believers in Jesus never want to feel as though they are compromising their doctrinal purity for social or political correctness. Therefore a rule of thumb that may help churches is to engage only in those cultural celebrations that do not contradict the values of the Christian faith. Other than that, the sky is the limit as long as the church keeps Christ at the core.

When our church has hosted international food festivals and multicultural dinners, we have exposed our people to the richness of other cultures that they may not have experienced before. They taste foods, hear music, and learn aspects of people's lives that they would not have known simply by sitting next to someone from another culture in church.

I'll never forget our staff Christmas party one year where we highlighted multicultural cuisine that included two Korean soup dishes, an African American entrée (a.k.a. soul food), Puerto Rican and West African side dishes, followed by a European custard dessert. Our icebreaker was a cultural proficiency game in which staff members had to answer humorous questions in order to receive prizes throughout the night. The party was hosted at the large home of a Puerto Rican staff member. After the dinner, the tables were removed so we could dance. We were taught some salsa dance moves. Some of us learned more quickly than others. Some of us never learned. All of us had fun.

I'm also reminded of a Valentine's Day dinner Bridgeway hosted where professional ballroom dancers taught couples how to square dance. For many this was indeed a cultural experience. Celebrating in different ways, employing many different cultural ideas, is a fun way to do life together. Each year several of our members join for a Passover Seder in which they share in a Jewish meal to remember the cultural and spiritual lineage of Christ. Through various multicultural expressions we experience God in ways that we would not otherwise have the privilege of doing. Rejoicing with others can be quite entertaining.

MULTICULTURAL VOICE BOXES

Consistent representation is a form of ongoing celebration. Out of the many speakers who teach from the platform on Sundays at Bridgeway, we have worked hard to bring a vast diversity of messengers to deliver the sermon. Each culture represented adds layers of color, variety, and styles in communication. From a prophetic preaching, to didactic teaching, to a comedic conversational style, Bridgeway tries to consistently feed the body good soul food. I'm sure there are times when we do not hit the mark, but we do try. Our commitment to lifting up diverse voices is not done as tokenism, which might only inspire a leader to invite a woman to speak on Mother's Day or an African American on MLK weekend. But instead, I intentionally share my pulpit in order to invite the gift that diverse voices infuse into the culture of our body. Just this past year, I have shared my pulpit with over twenty different people on Sunday mornings, which I know is very uncommon for a senior pastor to do. I do this because I know that in order to champion the voices and values of different ethnicities within our body, I cannot limit my congregation to allow only one cultural perspective to speak. Just in this ministry year alone our speakers have been white, black, Latino, Korean, and Albanian; men, women, Republican, Democrat, and Independent; and people in their 20s, 30s, 40s, 50s, 60s, and 70s. And that is just on Sunday mornings. If we talk about other Bible studies, midweek services, and special events, you would be hard-pressed to find anyone left out.

When the Holy Spirit choreographs unity at our church, he has available to him people from various preferences and styles, cultures, races, and genders. It is beautiful to watch God combine the parts of his body just as he imagined. By having a Korean preacher give the Word, Koreans are honored. Having a Filipino on stage to act out a lead role in a drama sketch communicates to Filipinos and others from the AAPI community that they have a stake in this ministry. When a Puerto Rican preaches, Latinos rejoice. When a woman teaches, half our population is lifted high. We believe that our culturally diverse population is celebrated by representation.

Minority representation, particularly in positions of leadership and influence, brings a sense of rejoicing to minority populations that the majority may sometimes overlook. Celebrating this kind of achievement, access, and the elevation of other groups is a practical way to enter into the joy of others.

Regardless of race or gender, when one adds the distinctions of diversity to the mouthpieces of the church, it broadens the styles and perspectives of God's Word being taught to his blended body. God clearly speaks through different voice boxes. Those men and women whom he speaks through come in different colors and from different cultures.

MULTICULTURAL WORSHIP

Hearing the Word of God through multicultural voice boxes is one thing, but celebrating in worship together with people from dozens of nations is breathtaking. The ultimate celebration of Christians is not the celebration of each other's culture, but rather occurs when all of those cultures unite at the foot of the cross and sing at the top of their lungs, "Holy, Holy, Holy is the Lord God Almighty."

When from the depths of our hearts we sing in unison "Great is Thy Faithfulness," worshiping God together is the most awesome celebration of all. I can't imagine what it must feel like to God, and look like to the angels, to witness a multicultural legion of worshipers lifting up the name of Jesus as Lord and King from the bottom of their hearts.

It is out of this kind of worship that we honor one another. As one body joined under one head, Jesus Christ, and out of our commitment to Christ and love for one another, we rejoice with those who rejoice.

Can you say, "I will celebrate with you" to others in your church? Whether it is someone in your small group who lands a new job, a woman who has a new baby, someone who has been blessed financially, or a racial group that achieves a significant social milestone? Saying "I will celebrate with you" adds to the unity of the church and counteracts resentment, bitterness, jealousy, and covetousness.

MISSING PIECE

I love Paul's summary statement that puts a stake in the ground and exclaims, "Now you are the body of Christ, and each one of you is a part of it" (1 Corinthians 12:27). That says it all, doesn't it?

We are all a part of God's kingdom puzzle. Each piece of a puzzle is essential. Have you ever put a puzzle together and discovered that one or two pieces were missing? I put together a one-hundred-piece puzzle with my son a number of years ago, but we only had ninety-nine pieces. That one missing piece drove us crazy! Finally, after searching in every possible place, we found that one little piece on the floor. Ah, now we were able to rest because the puzzle was complete. Whether the puzzle piece is big or small, an inside or a corner piece, a colorful or a monochrome piece, it is essential to completing the picture of the puzzle.

That same year I gave each of my staff members a puzzle-shaped pin they could wear to signify that each of us is an important piece of the body of Christ in general and an essential piece of the Bridgeway Community Church puzzle in particular. The message is a simple one—we are linked as one and we need each other.

Likewise Paul declared that we are all a part of God's kingdom puzzle and that everyone in our community of believers is a part of it too. The church down the street is a puzzle piece, as is the one on the other side of town. There is no part of the body, no piece of the puzzle, that is expendable or dispensable. Therefore let us refuse to treat anyone as if he or she doesn't matter. Each person's perspective, gifts, history, and experiences matter to God and should matter to us. When talking about bringing his whole self into his ministry leadership, my African American worship minister said just a few weeks ago, "You can't have diversity without me." I want to second that and say the same thing about each one of you reading this as well. We can't have diversity without you.

WHITE PIECES

As it relates to racial reconciliation, whites must have a place where they can voice their fears and ideas as well. They are a piece of God's diversity puzzle and should not be squeezed out of the celebration of multicultural unity. Oftentimes, in a culture that is quick to cancel, we cut short our opportunities to dig deep into the authentic feelings and unpolished thoughts that our white brothers and sisters wrestle through. They can feel as if they cannot share about the times they got it wrong or process through toxic thinking that might have been passed down to them from their parents or their community. Strategically boycotting or putting up healthy relational boundaries can still be integrated into our work as we seek racial justice. Some of our greatest achievements in racial advancement have leveraged this approach. However, let us choose to wield the weapon of this kind of social consequence with selective wisdom and not as our first line of defense. Cancel culture does deliver punishment for harmful actions, but it also can cut short honest dialogue that can lead to celebratory moments of transformation.

When I was teaching a cultural diversity course to working adults seeking their college degrees at the University of Phoenix, I asked my class if they wanted to read one of the letters from the manuscript of a book I was writing at the time, *Letters Across the Divide*. This book was a compilation of letters between a white businessman named Brent Zuercher, and me, a black pastor. For three years, from Chicago to Maryland, Brent and I dealt honestly with issues of race in our relationship via letters. Brent's questions to me, such as "Why is everything a racial issue for blacks?" "Why do I have to call you African American?" and "Who should apologize?" were the types of questions we discussed and debated. One evening in class we read the letter dealing with the question "Why are blacks so angry?" A white woman, Diana, read Brent's letter addressed to me, and then Tanya, a black woman, was assigned to read my response to Brent aloud, after which the class was to have an open discussion about what was read.

After Diana read Brent's letter to me in front of the class, an interesting twist of emotion took place. Brent's letter stated something to the effect of "I'm sick and tired of black preachers fanning flames of hate from their pulpits, and I'm exhausted by blacks crying wolf and whining about racism all the time. Love, Brent."

When Diana had finished reading this, the multicultural class of fifteen adults was silent. You could hear a pin drop in the room. Before moving on I acknowledged the awkwardness and asked the class what they were feeling. The woman who had just read Brent's letter began to shake. Her face began to flush red as tears welled up in her eyes and began to stream down her cheeks. "Diana," I said, "what's making you emotional?"

She responded in a stuttering fashion, as if to catch her breath from crying, "This is the way I feel."

Diana was a champion for diversity in her company and never saw herself as culturally incompetent. However, she never had her deeper thoughts expressed, validated, or even elevated to a question. She didn't know that anyone could actually express thoughts out loud like Brent did and not immediately be carted off as a racist. Brent was able to write these letters because of the safety of our friendship. Many whites don't have a venue where they can test their thoughts, ask their questions, communicate their objections, or voice their frustrations. Without such a forum, learning will not take place and comprehension will be aborted by a stronger resolve to resist change. In the forum of this classroom a safe place had been established, and Diana recognized through it that she had deeper unspoken feelings that Brent was unearthing.

The most beautiful thing was what happened next. Tanya, the African American woman assigned to read my letter of response to Brent, set down her papers, walked over to Diana, and hugged the white woman tightly. As they held each other, crying, the entire secular classroom became emotional. What a beautiful snapshot of reconciliation! A black woman and a white woman hugging as a way of communicating hurt, forgiveness, pain, comfort, understanding, and acceptance was a moment to remember. It was a special moment for our class. The barriers were down and real conversation erupted. No one was muted. The learnings, progress, and transformation of those white folks could then be celebrated by everyone in the room in a way that we would have never reached if Diana had been immediately canceled or shut down. The white experience was a puzzle piece that couldn't be left on the floor. As a gracist I must let whites know that they are a part of the multicultural body of Christ, lest they think that multicultural means everyone else but them. Every piece of the puzzle matters.

UNEARTHING YOUR DIVERSITY STORY

Everyone has a diversity story. Whether white, black, brown, red, or yellow, we all have a story. To unearth it, questions like the following are good discussion starters:

- When did you realize that you were different from others?
- When did you realize there was a race problem in society?
- How has growing up with no diversity affected your view of diverse people?

One of the ways of communicating to others that they matter to us is listening to their stories. Opening the door to multicultural dialogue provides space for storytelling. This can be done in small groups, during Bible studies, or even at multicultural fellowship dinners hosted between churches. All that is needed is a vision and a desire to have such a gathering with an open Bible, an open mind, and hearts that are open to listen and love. The Holy Spirit delights in guiding these kinds of gatherings in order to reveal God's bigger story of redemption and reconciliation. He wants to help us to be answers to Jesus' prayer for unity, one puzzle piece at a time.

11

Saying Eight:
I WILL HEAL WITH YOU

If one part suffers, every part suffers with it.

1 CORINTHIANS 12:26 (EMPHASIS ADDED)

For nearly two decades, the seven sayings of a gracist found in the original book *Gracism: The Art of Inclusion*, have been principles upon which many individuals, organizations, and governments have built bridges of peace, understanding, and reconciliation. But something vital broke inside our collective society, beginning in the year 2020 when we experienced a unique time of increased and intensified pain and division. From the deaths of a million people around the world because of the Covid-19 pandemic; to the horrific killing of George Floyd, an unarmed black citizen in Minneapolis, Minnesota, who died under the knee of a white police officer, Derek Chauvin; to the political attack of the US Capitol on January 6, 2021, when mobs of angry citizens sought to overturn the national presidential election of 2020 in America—our world has increasingly been "on tilt."

ON TILT

On tilt. Are you familiar with that phrase? If you know any-thing about pinball machines, then you know exactly what I'm talking about. While younger generations may not know much about pinball machines, these electronic gaming mechanisms from the 1970s and 1980s provided many hours of fun to teen-agers, like me, who frequented arcades back then. A little metal ball would bounce within a waist-high, standalone ma-chine, as the player would flick small rubber levers to push the ball around the machine for as long as possible to score points. If the player got too aggressive and physically shook the ma-chine too hard, the pinball machine would pause and halt the game with a flashing sign that indicated that it had gone "on tilt" and was inoperable for a short period. Almost immedi-ately, the player would slap the side of the machine because everything came to a halt and no progress was made in the game. For you younger folk, just imagine if you were right in the middle of a video game and your screen completely froze or the video started to buffer . . . it's that level of frustration.

Just like the pinball machine, our world has been shaken. One crisis right after another. It has become increasingly dif-ficult to make progress in the areas of reconciliation, peace, and bridge building as many have become numb or have grown cold by the overwhelming weariness of political and social discord. Our North American culture has seemingly gone on tilt!

Globally, we are witnessing callous and mind-numbing signs of stressful tilt as well. On February 24, 2022, Russia invaded Ukraine and began bombing innocent civilians. Cit-izens and NGO's throughout the rest of the world stepped up to assist refugees who were escaping the war-torn country of Ukraine. Governments found themselves trying to make sense of their relationship with Russia, oil supply issues, inflicting sanctions, strained food supply delivery, and a host of other subsequent ripple effects. The pinball machine of life seems chaotic enough on its own, but when it begins to get shaken by war, inflation, racial tension, gun violence, mass shootings, and refugee crises from Afghanistan, Central America, and now Ukraine, it's as if the whole world is on tilt.

As if all of that was not enough, in the summer of 2022, the US Supreme Court released their decision on one of the most divisive, controversial, and intractable ideological conflicts in our modern society. The overturning of *Roe v. Wade*, which gave power back to the states to ban, limit, or allow abortions, brought even more unrest and division. Pro-life advocates celebrated a long-awaited victory for the protection of the unborn. In stark contrast, pro-choice advocates felt personally violated in a way that only the most extreme language could capture. Although the pro-life movement has for the past fifty years attempted to convince their opposition that a pregnant woman has an uncontestable responsibility to bring her pregnancy to term, it was evident that their decades-long messaging had done little to nothing to win over the pro-choice populace. The mourning of the loss of body autonomy and fear of the deadly rise of nonmedical abortions took center stage that some claimed set our country back a half a century. *Tilt.*

With every additional event that shakes this world two things happen:

- Progress in bridge building halts
- Suffering in isolation heightens

SUFFER WITH EACH OTHER

As we have explored throughout this book thus far, we are taught in the Scriptures that, together, we as believers are one body made up of many parts. In the original edition of *Gracism—The Art of Inclusion*, I wrote about the seven sayings of a gracist that you have read about up to this point; I ended with the phrase found in verse 26 that focuses on rejoicing. The seventh saying is, "I will celebrate with you."

However, the first part of that verse gives us another exhortation that I believe is critical for the times we are in right now. It says, "If one part suffers, every part suffers with it" (1 Corinthians 12:26). The writer of the book of Corinthians, the apostle Paul, states that the evidence of the believers' unity is that they suffer along with each other. We are called to suffer with our brothers and sisters in Christ when they are experiencing harm, pain, or injury.

What if the bridge-building tool that we have been missing in the midst of this extreme unrest and tilt was right there all along? *Empathy*; suffering with those that suffer.

While belonging to the body of Christ, there are times when people from different backgrounds and identities find themselves in great pain. The gracist in the room is the one who empathizes with that pain and elects to walk empathetically with the injured party, regardless of their religious traditions, background, or philosophy. This means that a gracist may not always agree with someone else's choices or even understand the intricacies of their pain. The only thing they need to understand is that the other person is in pain. They understand that a community of people, whether LGBTQ+ communities, or women, or the poor, or other sociological groups, may feel hurt, damage, injury, or terror. The gracist acknowledges, empathizes, and draws close to those who bear the burden of hurt and harm.

Now, what moves this instruction beyond traditional empathy to gracist bridge building is when we remind ourselves how the writer began this passage. Earlier on in 1 Corinthians 12, as we are being told that the body is one unit although it has many parts, the writer targets these principles to address the distinctions of race and class. Paul says, "Whether Jews or Gentiles, slave or free . . . we were all given the one Spirit to drink" (v. 13). This passage reminds us that even though we may be different in background, class, and culture, we still belong to each other. No matter what label, distinction, or disagreement might separate us, we are one, and we are called to empathize with the other's pain and suffer alongside them.

SUPREME COURT OF PAIN

Is this type of gracism-empathy strong enough to bridge the divide between pro-life and pro-choice camps? When the Supreme Court ruled on June 24, 2022, to revert decision-making power to the states to limit abortions, it caused a lot of pain for women in our country. I will never forget the conversation I had with a woman who was very upset. Let's call her Lisa. Lisa was fearful, angry, and heartbroken over the Supreme Court decision. She described to me that even though she has a young son, she felt empowered to make the decision to carry him to term and give birth. The way she spoke of him I could tell that he is a great joy to his mother. Yet Lisa feared that if she were to get pregnant again, she would no longer have the power to choose as she did before whether or not to keep the new pregnancy and raise that child. She felt that her decision-making power was being stripped from her by a bunch of male (and one female) justices on the Supreme Court who should not have power over a woman's body. She felt that equality for women had just been set back fifty years.

She wanted me to speak up. She wanted me to say something about all this on social media. It is not uncommon for someone to ask me to release a statement on social media about an issue that is important to them. While I can't address every issue that surfaces in our society, Lisa's description of her anguish hit me in a powerful way. In her pain I felt the pain of so many others, and I knew I could not look past her and dismiss her request. Now, Lisa knows that I am a male, pro-life pastor and that I prefer that, in most cases, a conceived child should be born. However, she wanted me to know the great distress and fear many women like her were experiencing. She wanted me to know the cascading emotions that were triggered by the court ruling and that such a personal decision about abortion should be made privately in limited ways without being criminalized.

Typically, throughout the years, the way conservative pro-life evangelicals have been encouraged to respond in this situation is to point out our disagreements, make bold claims about life beginning at conception, and try to convince Lisa to change her views. We have tried that method for decades. We often disregard the person's fears and minimize the importance of their claims that they feel a violation of bodily autonomy. We do not suffer with those that suffer, but instead we silence those that suffer. Somewhere along the way we have given ourselves permission to look past the woman and only see the unborn. I was determined not to do that.

I took time to slow down and feel this pain along with my sister in Christ. I was committed to not dismissing her feelings and along with them the feelings of millions of other women who shared her pain. No one would have been surprised if I were to have been unyielding, but instead, I allowed myself to begin to feel conflicted. I wondered what it would feel like to have the government force me to give birth if a child were growing in my body. Below is what I posted on social media to demonstrate care beyond my own understanding, confliction, convictions, or preferences:

> I feel sad for many women who know that a bunch of men who can do what they want sexually can impregnate a woman & walk away while she's forced to give birth & raise the child with no consequences to him who engaged in the behavior. As a pro-life male pastor, I feel her pain.

After my post I received many responses on and off social media. Some said that no one who supports abortion can be a follower of Jesus Christ.

Therein lies the difference between gracism and a lack thereof. In my post and the reactions, you have two pro-life perspectives: My post attempted to harness the empathy of gracism; some of the other reactions were devoid of empathy or care for those who hold a different view. They were judgmental, accusatory, and frankly mean.

When it comes to empathy, we are called as followers of Jesus Christ to feel so we can help heal. Whether I agree or disagree with another's position, as a gracist I refuse to dismiss the pain and perspective of others and withhold a desire to understand. How often do we push people away from Christ because we look past them and only put our eyes on an issue that we believe we have already figured out?

Paul teaches elsewhere that we who are believers share in the suffering and in the glory of Christ. He says this: "Now if we are children, then we are heirs—heirs of God and co-heirs with Christ, if indeed we share in his sufferings in order that we may also share in his glory" (Romans 8:17). In the same way, we are to share in the sufferings of our brothers and sisters in Christ, even if we do not understand or know them. Dismissing Lisa as one who does not follow the Messiah, like responses to my post expressed, just makes it easier for someone to dismiss the pain of women, or anyone's pain for that matter, about anything.

IS THE ASH HEAP METHOD WORKING?

While it may be easier to discount the feelings of others with whom you disagree by flinging them onto the ash heap of unbelief or atheism, what do you do when you have Christ-followers who feel differently than you do? What do you do with LGBTQ+ believers in Christ who worship the same God as you? Do you just fling them all onto the ash heap of apostasy? What do you do with pro-choice believers in Christ who worship the same God as you? Ash heap?

Is throwing everyone who disagrees with our traditional view of Scripture into the category of unbelievers or apostates the best way to sanitize our views and anesthetize ourselves from caring about what others think and feel?

Many Christian Republicans have written off pro-choice Democrats as unbelievers because of their position on abortion and their refusal to protect the life of the unborn child in the womb. In addition, in the mind of many Republicans, Christian sexual ethics leave no room for LGBTQ+ relationships according to Scripture: therefore, one cannot be a true believer and a Democrat at the same time. As gracists, however, we must teach that "ash heap" responses do not bring about understanding or healing. In similar fashion, many Democrats who are believers in Christ have thrown many white evangelical Christians onto the ash heap because of their unwavering support for former President Donald Trump. Black people, in particular, are fed up with evangelicals' refusal to believe that many people of color feel the deep pain of racism as a reality and not just a sneaky way of indoctrinating children with critical race theory (CRT). Also, because many people of color have a difficult time reconciling the presence of modern-day racism within modern-day Christianity, it is tempting for them to fling whites onto the ash heap of irrelevant and inauthentic Christianity. When government programs for the poor, the immigrant, and the social outcasts in society are cut while tax breaks are given to the rich, it is difficult for Democrats to reconcile why any true believer in Jesus Christ would balk at attempts to bail out the economic underclass. Jesus lived among the poor, and yet many evangelicals who claim his name are seemingly more passionate about protecting gun rights and lobbying for corporate bailouts for businesses and billionaires. Are any of these arguments good enough reason to throw a person out of the family of Christ and onto the ash heap of unbelief?

If we get in the business of writing off everyone with whom we disagree or don't understand as "unbelievers," then it will be very hard to be a gracist, because inherent in gracism is the call to empathy and healing. Disagreement on political issues, platforms, and ideologies will always happen within as well as outside the body of Christ. I know that it is especially difficult when these mindsets produce harmful results for others. But the way believers engage these issues and the spirit of empathy with which they engage them, is what marks the difference between those who are gracists and those who are not.

I WILL HEAL WITH YOU

When I empathize with others who are in pain, I am sharing in their suffering by caring about how they feel. Gracism means to extend favor, even when others are struggling through terrible difficulties in life, difficulties with which we cannot relate or even fully understand. While racial strife and many other forms of injury hurt the hearts of people we live and worship with, sharing in the pain of others demonstrates that in the midst of the divide, we care.

The bonus saying of a gracist—the eighth saying if you will—is this: "I will heal with you." This means I will walk with you through your pain. I will listen, learn, experience, and imagine the hurt that you must be feeling. I am willing to walk with you on the path of healing and share in the burdens of carrying your cross alongside you. If I can feel with you, then I can heal with you.

SUFFERING ALONE

Dave Heiliger is a white brother who is the pastor of multicultural bridge building at Bridgeway Community Church in Maryland where I serve as founding pastor. I have served in ministry with Dave and mentored him in race relations for about a decade. He is a Bible college graduate and holds a master's degree in peacebuilding and conflict transformation. Therefore, I am always eager to talk with Dave about matters of reconciliation and bridge building. When discussing the concepts of suffering, empathy, and healing as the eighth saying of a gracist, Dave said to me:

> As we talk about gracism, we say that it is a positive solution to a negative problem. It's something positive you can "do" to address racism. However, suffering does not seem like the kind of positive solution that the other seven sayings embody. One of the reasons I could see people bypass suffering with others is because it doesn't sound positive or constructive. When suffering is thrust on us, we try to get past it as quickly as possible. For

many of us, when we think back to our times of deepest suffering it carries feelings of regret, anger, unanswered questions, abuse, and trauma. Why would anyone willingly enter a time of suffering or see it as a solution? There is nothing positive about this solution.

That is until we view it from the other side. There is only one thing worse than suffering—and that is suffering in isolation. The positive perspective of this seemingly not so positive approach is remembering how meaningful it is, for the person who is suffering, to be met in their pain by a loving friend. Instead of immediately asking "What can I do" or rushing to fix a problem, suffering with someone else who is suffering offers a healing presence that no amount of action or activism alone can match.

When we grieve with someone who is grieving, we demonstrate a depth of commitment to that person in his or her deepest time of need. As another pastor on our ministry team often says, "You can fake a lot of things, but you can't fake showing up."

The pain that is brought on by racial abuse is not similar to that caused by a mere scratch or bump; it cannot be made better with a kiss and a bandage or the grown-up version of that, a mere offering of "thoughts and prayers." Instead, for the type of pain that is wrapped up in cycles of injustice, historical harm, and community struggle, we have to engage in actions that will help mend broken bones. We must triage deep injuries that come from the trauma of seeing unexpected mass shootings, police brutality, innocent Asians becoming victims of violence, and the rise of white supremacy groups like the Oath Keepers, Proud Boys, the 3 Percenters, and a host of other militia groups including the Ku Klux Klan.

Empathy in this must not resemble pity. It must not be limited to emotional empathy. There is an experiential empathy and sacrificial engagement that comes with the charge to "suffer with." The privileged person elects to come close and feel the pain along with their brother or sister, and then out of that connection leverages their own time, money, and advocacy and maximizes their platform for justice. I will heal with you means I will feel with you. It also means that I will engage in actions and sacrifice that will demonstrate that I am willing to be real with you about change.

A WEARY WHITE FRIEND

I have had many white friends, family members, and church members show up for me in my time of hurt. I am so grateful to be a part of a multicultural church family, and I enjoy having people from many different ethnic backgrounds in my life.

Sadly, there are also times when people let you down. I am sure you and I have let others down when they were counting on us. However, when layers of racial tension are added to the mix, wounds seem to cut deeper.

After more than thirty years journeying toward racial reconciliation, I could not believe the reversal of heart and attitudes that many of my dear white friends developed between the years of 2016 through 2020. One friend and I had regular conversations for years about matters of racial justice. He is a white brother who wanted to learn, grow, empathize, and make things better in the world as it related to the racial division and brokenness. But the brokenness of the world broke something in him.

We had not talked about such matters of race or shared perspectives on different episodes of injustice for a while. I guess life became busy and we were all focused on our own families and ministries; that happens. Nevertheless, once the world was seemingly "on tilt," after the George Floyd murder, I was sure my friend was going to check up on me and check in with me, but sadly, he never did. To my surprise, months went by, then a year. Then another six months.

As I was pastoring thousands of people in a multicultural ministry trying to survive the divisiveness of those painfully toxic years and the effect it was having on my congregation, I, too, had to figure out my own emotions as an African American male. I was feeling choked by the images, news reports, and replays of George Floyd's heartbreaking death as he was slowly being killed with Officer Chauvin's knee on his neck. It was disheartening to hear the verbal jabs of white political figures and everyday Americans who cheered on the harsh rhetoric against those who protested racial injustice against unarmed black people.

Equally as painful was to hear white leaders discount and dismiss the cries of racism by NFL players, black entertainment personalities, or everyday black people who were struggling with personal trauma and mental anguish every time another unarmed black person was killed. At this time, many white evangelical church leaders used their platforms to herald their opposition to critical race theory and openly declared white supremacy as a fallacy, all while elevating the president of the United States at that time as an anointed savior of America. For every congregation openly supporting the president, countless others remained silent from the pulpits, while thousands of African Americans were dying a slow and painful death emotionally, mentally, and spiritually right in the pews of their churches. Indeed, many African Americans who had been attenders and members of multiethnic churches across the country found the silence of their spiritual leaders deafening.

As they entered the doors of their churches each Sunday seeking solace and comfort from their pastor, they were instead met with an inability or unwillingness to even mention the racial tension boiling over in the country. As a result, many people of color found it necessary for their own spiritual and mental health to walk away from a ministry that had nurtured them for years. Some left quietly, not notifying clergy of their departure. Others left loud—they made sure their pastors knew *exactly* why they chose to part ways.

Gratefully, I had many other quality relationships with white brothers and sisters that brought healing and gave me emotional oxygen during this seemingly suffocating season. Thankfully, my hope was not dependent on this one relationship with the white brother that had gone completely silent. By God's grace, years of multicultural relationships with people from other cultures carried me through this crippling era of multicultural leadership. Still, what was it about this one white friend that caused him to go completely radio silent? What was keeping *me* from reaching out to *him*?

BOARD MEETING REVELATION

While sitting in a board meeting one day for the diversity consulting organization I run called Gracism Global, an African American board member was telling a story about a relationship he had with a white friend who had disappointed him by going silent and refusing to discuss matters of race with him. This board member was admitting that he felt convicted to reach out to that white friend as a gracist. Even though as a black man he himself was in pain, he knew that reconciliation could only come if he took the initiative. He admitted, like many people of color do, that it is very exhausting to have to take the initiative repeatedly when it comes to racial justice and reconciliation issues. However, this board member did so and shared with us that he chose to obey the Lord, who had been bringing this matter to his conscience.

As I was listening to this board member's reflection, I began to feel convicted by my own lack of initiative in the relationship I had with my white friend who had not reached out to me. As a result, I committed to reaching out. Days later, I picked up the phone and sent a text to my friend. Let's call him Chuck.

Chuck responded with a long explanation of the pain he himself had been going through personally and spiritually. He apologized for not being present, for not reaching out, and promised to write to me to explain more about his inability to be empathetic. Weeks later Chuck's long-awaited email arrived explaining that he was not in a good emotional place and was sick and tired that society had blamed him for every social ill of the day just because he was a white man.

Chuck said he was beaten down by the fact that he was constantly confronted with feelings of failure. Failure in his marriage, failure in his faith, and failure when it came to race relations, although he had previously demonstrated growth and understanding in this area for years. In other words, Chuck was exhausted by the topic of race and expressed his dismay at being the target of society's blame and ire. Hence, Chuck went missing emotionally and went silent relationally.

Some may call this a cop-out. Others may call it fragility. However, the ability to handle such stress with resilience is not as easy as some might think. While many African Americans are beyond exhaustion, and there is absolutely no comparison of the pain that blacks have endured from the victimization and violence they've experienced over centuries, the mental toll that racism has had on white people cannot be dismissed either.

JAILHOUSE ROCK

Do you remember the biblical story of Paul and Silas in prison in Acts 16? While incarcerated, the praise songs they lifted up to God shook the foundations of the prison. Miraculously, the prison doors flung open. Paul and Silas were free to go. Do you remember what the jailer who was on guard that night was about to do to himself?

He was about to fall on his sword and kill himself because he had failed to guard the prisoners. Paul and Silas stopped him and shared the good news with him about the love and power of Jesus Christ. That day the jailer and his family discovered the gracious favor of God and were saved by the gospel.

Here is the point: When the chains of injustice fall and the foundations of the prisons of racism are shaken at the core, not only are those who suffer injustice freed, like Paul and Silas were, but the ones that inflict or ignore that injustice are freed as well. The jailer was the oppressor in this story. Even if he was not doing so in his heart, even if he was not the one to set the rules, even if he was simply "following orders," he was on the side of oppression. His job and his class demanded it. He was associated with the oppression of injustice whether by design or default. Nevertheless, once the injustice was broken, the jailer had a choice. Despair and surrender to his guilt, fear, and shame; or surrender to the grace of God to find hope, healing, deliverance, and freedom. He responded to God's grace.

When injustice is addressed and overcome, that freedom has the potential to effect healing not only for the oppressed but also for those who inflict or ignore the oppression. The ability to build our resilience beyond what some might call fragility is found when we surrender to the God of grace, who grants us the oxygen and energy to be resilient emotionally, spiritually, and relationally.

Although the process is turbulent, healing must begin with the shattering of dividing walls and the shaking of the prison foundations that have held the systems of racism in place. When the grace of God becomes the oxygen that empowers opposing parties to walk together, then true racial healing can take place. God's grace can give me the strength to hang in there with you, and you with me.

One may ask, "How can I heal with you when I need healing myself?"

The answer is this: I can heal with you only as I, myself, am being healed. I can empathize with you as I have someone to empathize with me. I am discovering that a multicultural community of wounded healers is the ingenious and intangible power of the eighth saying of a gracist, "I will heal with you."

The world may be on tilt, but God has the power to move it from tilt to a complete reckoning that shakes the very foundations to level ground. Yet, the rebuilding and healing of something new can rise up in a way that brings the flourishing of new life and new possibilities.

Empathy, caring, lament, suffering, and feeling each other's pain while striving to understand one another's struggle is the pathway to healing the deep wounds between us.

12

HOW CAN I BECOME A GRACIST?

In this book you have read that everyone has dots. We all have issues, experiences, gifts, and distinctions that must be integrated into the puzzle of the kingdom life. How do people from different backgrounds live together in unity within the body of Christ? How do we live out our faith beyond the walls of the body of Christ as part of the broader human family? I have highlighted eight sayings from Paul's words in 1 Corinthians that you can cling to as you struggle with what it means to be a reconciler in a divided world and church. Here are the sayings once again from 1 Corinthians 12:22-26:

1. "I will lift you up" (special honor, v. 23).

2. "I will cover you" (special modesty, v. 23).

3. "I will share with you" (no special treatment, v. 24).

4. "I will honor you" (greater honor, v. 24).

5. "I will stand with you" (no division, v. 25).

6. "I will consider you" (equal concern, v. 25).

7. "I will celebrate with you" (rejoices with, v. 26).

8. "I will heal with you" (suffers with, v. 26).

Imagine saying these phrases to your spouse, pastor, church leadership team, small group, family members, or a racial group that God lays on your heart. It is a powerful thing to say these phrases with a deep sense of personal commitment.

SPIRIT-LED COMMUNITY

Beyond individual commitment there is a communal commitment that brings all we have stated full circle. Paul spoke of the individual parts of the body as an interconnected and interlinked unit. These sayings, lived out in community through small groups, covenant groups, and support groups, bring to us the mutuality of interdependence that lifts us up as one. Christian community is essential to body life and is the container within which the Holy Spirit delights in moving.

In 1 Corinthians 12:4-6, Paul precedes the human body illustration by talking about the leadership of the Holy Spirit. This is one of only two times in the New Testament where the Holy Spirit is mentioned in the first position when referring to the triune God. Notice the text: "There are different kinds of gifts, but the same *Spirit* distributes them. There are different kinds of service, but the same *Lord*. There are different kinds of working, but in all of them and in everyone it is the same *God* at work" (emphasis added). The only other place in the New Testament where the third person of the Trinity is placed first is in Ephesians 4:4-6: "There is one body and one *Spirit*, just as you were called to one hope when you were called; one *Lord*, one faith, one baptism; one *God* and Father of all, who is over all and through all and in all" (emphasis added).

Don't you find it interesting that in both places in Scripture, the context of the Spirit's leadership is oneness? Both passages are speaking to the issue of unity through diversity. I truly believe that the unity of the body is a spiritual matter first and foremost. God's Spirit delights in breaking down barriers and adjoining different parts of the body—causing them to dance. The Holy Spirit is the breath within the body that gives life to all the parts. Even when Jesus prayed for the oneness of the church as recorded in John 17, he did so after the discourse of the Holy Spirit recorded in John 16. The Acts 2 passage that outlines the inauguration of the New Testament church is set off by the movement of the Holy Spirit among the diverse crowd of new believers.

My point is that it takes the movement of the Holy Spirit to work among the individual members, revealing to them their desperate need for one another. It seems to me that the Spirit's job is to move within a community, aligning, ordering, and interconnecting various parts of the body to ease their working together like oil moving within an engine or machine. When Spirit-led believers come together in communal interdependence, the Spirit maximizes kingdom potential and moves in dynamic and unpredictable ways. When believers come together in prayer and unity, the Spirit is invited to act.

I am reminded of the story of the dry bones in Ezekiel 37. God, in a dream, instructed Ezekiel to preach to a valley of dry bones, representing the need for the restoration of Israel. The breath and movement of the Spirit came after the bones in the valley were organized and put together. Preceding the organization of the bones in the valley was the prophetic preaching of Ezekiel. My hope is that this book, along with the messages of others who have been called to write and preach this message, will be a prophetic call for the church, like that addressed to the dry bones, to come together. When we move in that direction, the Spirit will lift the church to levels unseen in our divided world and churches.

BEGIN A GRACIST JOURNEY

As I stated in chapter two, gracism is the positive extension of favor to others regardless of and sometimes because of their color, class, or culture. The effects of racism can be wide-reaching in our society. That is why we need God-sized grace to overcome it; his grace is wide and all encompassing. In many ways, race and class are on-ramps to the broader highway of grace for many people if we choose to use it this way. Instead of using race, class, and culture as negative descriptors that cause us to resist one another, I challenge us to use these distinctives as opportunities to extend grace more fully—in gracism. I would add that this extension of favor must include all who are on the fringes regardless of their gifts, abilities, or distinctions. It is the call and responsibility of the majority to extend grace to the minority in all cases. By becoming a gracist, you will be more like Christ and will become a bridge builder for unity. Will you say yes to this call?

Below are some practical suggestions of what you can do to begin your gracist journey of reconciliation.

Receive the grace of God in your life first. The Bible is clear that we have all sinned and have fallen way short of reaching God's standard of perfection (Romans 3:23). Our sinful condition causes all of us to be separated from God (death) and forever lost in our waywardness (Romans 6:23). Because of his grace, God has purposefully reached out to build a bridge to the human race and has offered salvation from eternal separation and forgiveness of sin. Such love can come only from God. He loves you and me so much that he extends his gracious hand toward each of us (John 3:16). All we have to do is accept his unbelievable proposal.

If you have not given your RSVP to God's loving proposal to forgive you for your sin and begin a personal relationship of trust with him, then now is the time for you to respond to God. Pause right now, close your eyes, and picture God on one knee extending to you his divine hand of proposal. Will you pray and say to God, "I do"? Tell him that you accept his proposal to forgive you and walk with you forever in a relationship. Ask God to forgive you. Ask him to come into your life and be your Lord and Savior. Pray in faith and believe that you are forgiven and cleansed. God promises to respond to your cry and hear your prayer even now (Romans 10:13).

You may want to say a prayer to God like the one below, or using a similar one using your own words:

> Dear God, I know that I am a sinner who is separated from you. I know that I need a Savior; and Jesus Christ, you are him. I invite you into my life today to be my Lord and Savior. Please forgive me for my sin. I choose to follow you by faith today. I believe in you. I accept your divine proposal to forgive me and walk with me forever. I give my life to you now. In Jesus' name, amen.

If you prayed the above prayer with a sincere heart, the Bible promises that you are saved (Romans 10:9-10, 13). The next step for you is to find a church family or a community of believers who can help you grow in your faith. If you have a Christian friend or family member, contact that person and tell him or her about what you just prayed. It will encourage that person, and hopefully she or he will be able to help you along the way in your faith. Feel free to email me personally through my website at bridgeway.cc and let me know that you prayed this prayer. I will do my best to help you find a church or get some material in your hands to help you in your journey. I want to hear from you.

If you have already received Christ as your Lord and Savior, then you are a personal example and recipient of God's grace. Are you now ready to extend it to others?

Reach over the color line by inviting someone to your church or home. If you are a Christian, let me encourage you to invite someone who is on the other side of the racial, ethnic, or economic divide to your church, small group, or home this month. Please don't do this for my sake, but do it for God's sake. This is what the body of Christ is to be. God's children are from every color, class, and culture. For example, if you are black, I encourage you to invite a white or Hispanic person to your church or home. If you are white, invite a black person to your church or home. If you are Vietnamese, why not invite a non-Asian over for dinner? If you are Puerto Rican, reach out to a Mexican and build a friendship. This is where concept and reality intersect from theory to practical life.

Christianity at its best is a faith that reaches across lines of comfort and convenience (Acts 1:8). It is a faith that follows the model of its founder, Jesus Christ, who gave up the prerogatives of his divine nature and became a humble and obedient servant as a man (Philippians 2:6-8). He did this not for a one-time dinner date, but for an everlasting relationship. Maybe a small group atmosphere where you can mix with people from other backgrounds will help you become comfortable with others as a step toward spending alone time with them over coffee or dinner. Is there a family in your Sunday school class, Bible study meeting, or weekly fellowship group whom you might be able to engage in conversation? Why not begin there and see what God does through your faith? He desires for gracism to work more than we do. I promise that he will come through.

Read on the subject of reconciliation. Another way to grow as a new gracist is to read on subjects that help you understand the culture, plight, and history of other ethnic and racial groups. I have found that most bridge builders are people who are learners and not know-it-alls. It takes great effort to read and learn about other people whom you have no need to know in order to survive or succeed. Electing to do so is an act of love and will speak volumes to those about whom you learn.

I commend my previous books, *Letters Across the Divide* and *Multicultural Ministry* to you. I hope you will read these if you have not done so already; they will help you build racial bridges in life and ministry. While this may sound a bit self-promotional, my heart has vested much into these works, and I believe they will serve you well. In addition many others have invested their lives, ministries, and intellects into reconciliation, Christian unity, and aspects of multicultural ministry that can be extremely helpful to learners as well. Please see my reading list at the end of the book.

Relate on purpose to people who are different. Make it your business to shop, work out, eat, or play in parts of town where you have a higher probability of interacting with people who are different from you. I know this may seem far-fetched and out of the way, but think of how far Christ came to build a relationship with us on earth. Think how Jesus purposed to walk through Samaria to meet the Samaritan woman at the well. If we don't purpose to relate to others whom we can easily ignore, we will miss the blessings of gracism. In reaching out, we will reap the wonderful learning that comes—namely, that we ourselves have been reached and blessed in ways we never knew. When we seek to include, we discover that the very ones we reached out to have something we are missing. There is a piece of God that we lack when we exclude others who reflect something of him that we could not in any other way see.

If you are already interacting with folks that are different from you on a peer level, take it to the next step and begin to serve under the leadership of a person who is from a minority group that is not your own. Do not seek to rise in the ranks of leadership; do not try to get the organization to do things your way. Simply begin to put in the hours, days, energy, and sweat to do the jobs that are assigned to you, in order to support that leader as they lead the way to achieve the goals they are reaching for. In submitting to the leadership of a person like this you will bless them and the community around them as they succeed.

Link with a church or organization that promotes care for the poor. It is imperative that we join hands with others who seek to relieve oppression, racism, poverty, and hunger. Our Lord clearly illustrates that his followers are to demonstrate love and goodness to those less fortunate (Matthew 25:40). Do an online search for a ministry or nonprofit entity that you can support in your local area or around the world to be a part of the solution to suffering.

A CLOSING WORD

I end this book with an African proverb that has guided me in bridge building and racial healing. While I still have a long way to go, this proverb reminds me that dialogue begins the process of relating and respecting those who are different from me.

> When I saw him from afar, I thought he was a monster.
> When he got closer, I thought he was just an animal.
> When he got closer, I recognized that he was a human.
> When we were face-to-face, I realized that he was
>   my brother.

As long as we keep people at a distance, we can categorize them as monsters or animals. Distance demonizes. But when we get closer and begin to communicate with each other, we recognize that people are just like us in many ways. Comprehension begins with conversation. Essential to grace is a person who is willing to receive it, and then out of a grace-filled heart is compelled to extend it. May God bless you and keep you as you embrace, exemplify, and educate others about gracism.

QUESTIONS FOR REFLECTION AND DISCUSSION

1. EVERYONE HAS A DOT

1. Are you aware of your personal "red dot" (whatever makes you feel insecure around others, such as race, gender, age, weight, facial feature, emotional or physical disability)? How do you manage your feelings about it?

2. Do you sometimes try to overcompensate for your "red dot" when you relate to others, especially those who don't know you? If so, how?

3. Can you recall a time of discouragement or even despair over your "red dot"? What circumstances brought on those emotions?

4. Racism is a sin that can be committed by any identity group against another. How have you experienced someone making judgments about you because you were part of a certain identity group?

5. What are the factors that are helping our society to minimize dotism? What are the factors that are still promoting dotism? Which factors (one from each list) are the easiest for you to engage in?

2. FROM RACISM TO GRACISM

1. Can you think of an instance when you experienced favor—you were included in a positive way in what others were already experiencing? How did that giving of grace make you feel? How did you respond to those around you?

2. Can you think of a time where you were shown favoritism—others were excluded while you were included? How is your reaction to favoritism different from your reaction to favor?

3. Can you think of a time when you were excluded and others were shown favoritism? What was your reaction to that event?

4. Based on your knowledge of the Bible, do you think the authors' use of the term *gracism* is legitimate? Besides the example of Hagar used by the authors, what other biblical stories illustrate God's gracism?

5. Can you think of a situation where you acted like a gracist—one who sees, hears, or pays attention to people on the margins, extending positive ministry and service?

6. The authors admit that the exercise of gracism seems too simplistic an answer for the conflicts of race and culture in our world. Yet how could the exercise of gracism at the one-on-one level help the conflicts in your world?

3. THE ART OF INCLUSION

1. How have you seen the increase in minority populations where you live? List from three to five places or instances where you have noticed it.

2. If you have a Walmart or Target in your area, take an hour and sit in the snack or coffee bar and mark on a sheet of paper the different groups of people you are able to identify. What surprised you in this experiment? Besides English, how many other languages did you hear? How has this exercise supported or contradicted the authors' contention of increased cultural diversity?

3. Read 1 Corinthians 12 slowly. How does the inclusion of culture and class change how you apply this passage?

4. The authors stated, "A gracist can't help but think about those in the neighborhood who are of a different color than are the congregants." After your Walmart or Target experiment, compare your observations of the store's level of diversity of customers to the level of diversity of your church's congregation. Which is more diverse? Which institution, based on 1 Corinthians 12, should be more diverse? Why does this difference not bother most churches and their leaders? Should it bother them? Why or why not?

4. SAYING ONE: I WILL LIFT YOU UP

1. Within the walls of your church as it is now, who are the marginalized people who are not "in"? The poor? The less educated? The teenagers? The singles? Those divorced? Single mothers? Identify at least two marginalized groups within your church. How can you be an ambassador of reconciliation to that group? How can you educate yourself about them?

2. The authors state, "I have learned that the best way to avoid such embarrassing moments is to simply ask the best way to serve, inspire, help, or lift them." What is

one gift of kindness you could do for your prayer partner that would truly meet his or her need without causing humiliation?

3. Who are the people in your church who deserve special honor awards? Are there other people in your life— parents, spouses, neighbors, teachers—who deserve special honor awards? Buy a box of thank-you cards and one evening sit down to write special honor award notes.

4. Are there any people who you feel should be excluded from the circle of honor? Why?

5. Who are the people you usually are drawn to lift up? What is it about them that draws you? Are there other important characteristics that you might be excluding but that you should recognize?

5. SAYING TWO: I WILL COVER YOU

1. How much value does our society place on the virtue of modesty? How does this affect our ability to be sensitive to care for the modesty of others?

2. What biblical examples can you think of where one person in the power position did not embarrass or shame someone in a weaker position, but rather protected, cared for, or shielded that person?

3. How could exposing people hurt their spiritual growth? How could it help them? What are the standards you use to know which action to take?

4. Journal about an event in your past when someone else stood up for your reputation or protected you from others' judgment. What emotions did you feel?

6. SAYING THREE: I WILL SHARE WITH YOU

1. Why do we struggle with the choices of community versus comfort? What are the benefits of each? What are the downsides of each?

2. When have you either benefited from or been excluded from "getting a piece of the pie"? When you are on the benefit side, how do you feel? What behaviors do you have to engage in? When you are on the excluded side, how do you feel? What behaviors do you engage in? How does receiving benefits or being excluded affect relationships?

3. Have you ever benefited from "graceonomics"—the leveraging of financial and relational networks to help others succeed in their economic worlds? Are there people in your world whom you could help through graceonomics? What are some of the reasons others might not have financial and relational networks? What knowledge or skills would they need?

4. "Gracist living doesn't refuse the good things that life has to offer," the authors say. "It simply refuses to ignore those who aren't as privileged to enjoy such benefits and is committed to doing something about it." What are three commitments you can make today that will help you be more of a gracist? Tell someone else the commitments you have made.

7. SAYING FOUR: I WILL HONOR YOU

1. When does your fairness meter sound? Do you agree with the authors that grace is unfair? How has God's being unfair benefited you?

2. Spend a quiet time in Psalm 103. List all the benefits God extends to us. Use that list in your prayer time with God, thanking him for his unfairness to you.

3. "I now believe it is okay to be unfair," the authors state, "not for the purposes of hurting others, but for the purposes of helping those who are in a state of lack." Make a list of those in special need to whom our society extends grace (such as handicap parking). Why is the fairness factor with them not an issue?

4. What are some ways you can extend grace through service in your community?

5. When have you heard someone say something negative about a particular people group? What was your internal reaction? Did you respond to the people present there? If not you, did someone else? Write down a proactive response you can use at a future time when someone speaks negatively about a particular people group.

6. Of the five ways of extending grace—with my service, with my speech, with my stewardship, with my social media, with my sitting—which one is the easiest for you to engage in? Which one is the hardest for you? Why?

8. SAYING FIVE: I WILL STAND WITH YOU

1. How have you experienced the pain of division or conflict that led you and another, or you and a group, from continuing to be a part of each other's lives? What are some of the emotions that are stirred from that separation as you reflect on it today? What were the consequences of that division?

2. When have you experienced unity with another person or group of people? What emotions do you feel when strongly connected to others? What are the results that have come from the experience of unity for you, others, a church, or a group?

3. Read all three prayers of Jesus (Matthew 6:9-13; 26:39, 42; John 17). Write down the words and phrases from each prayer that you are especially drawn to. Read Revelation 5:6-14 and write down the words and phrases from that passage that you are drawn to. How are the lists from the passages different? How are they similar?

4. What was your response to the story in this chapter about serving Ukrainian refugees? What internal battles have you faced when considering how to stand with those in your community who express that they are facing injustice, oppression, or unequal challenges?

9. SAYING SIX: I WILL CONSIDER YOU

1. Write in a journal about any encounters you have had with the homeless or poor. What were your initial thoughts and feelings? How do you normally respond to the homeless?

2. What reasons would the Levite and priest in the good Samaritan story give for avoiding the man on the side of the road? How are those reasons similar to your responses in question one?

3. What do you think the reasons were for the good Samaritan to help the man who was robbed?

4. How do you want God to minister through you to those who are in need? Can you identify ways that

you might be able to position yourself to move in this direction?

10. SAYING SEVEN: I WILL CELEBRATE WITH YOU

1. Can you remember a time when it was difficult for you to rejoice with someone else? Share why it was hard.

2. While growing up, when did you realize that you were different from others? How are you still different? How does being different make you feel?

3. How do you view whites in the diversity conversation? If you are a white person, do you feel like you have a voice? Explain. If you are not white, do you feel like whites have something to offer when it comes to diversity? Why or why not?

11. SAYING EIGHT: I WILL HEAL WITH YOU

1. What difficulties have you faced in engaging in conversations across racial lines during this "on tilt" season of our nation?

2. If those from a different racial group than your own showed genuine self-sacrificial empathy toward you and the struggles of those in your racial group, how do you think that would advance the cause of healing?

3. Why do we sometimes struggle to show empathy? Can empathy be seen as a weakness? Do you think there are any negative associations with empathy?

4. Can you think of a time when someone saw you at a point of struggle and joined you in your pain so that

you would not be alone? What came as a result of their act of solidarity?

5. What group of people have you been taught to throw onto the "ash heap" of unbelief because of their stance on a certain issue? What is your biggest barrier to including them under the covering of God's grace?

6. What biblical examples can you think of where one person shows the empathy of gracism to another?

NOTES

INTRODUCTION

6   Gracism, *unlike racism*: David A. Anderson, *Multicultural Ministry: Finding Your Church's Unique Rhythm* (Grand Rapids, MI: Zondervan, 2004).

2. FROM RACISM TO GRACISM

18   *I define* gracism: David A. Anderson, *Multicultural Ministry: Finding Your Church's Unique Rhythm* (Grand Rapids, MI: Zondervan, 2004).

3. THE ART OF INCLUSION

30   *Almost 50 percent*: William H. Frey, "The US Will Become 'Minority White' in 2045, Census Projects," Brookings, March 14, 2018, www.brookings.edu/blog/the-avenue/2018/03/14/the-us-will-become-minority-white-in-2045-census-projects.
Three out of ten people: William H. Frey, "The Nation Is Diversifying Even Faster than Predicted, According to New Census Data," Brookings, July 1, 2020, www.brookings.edu/research/new-census-data-shows-the-nation-is-diversifying-even-faster-than-predicted.

31   *At the current rate*: Marlene L. Rossman, *Multicultural Marketing: Selling to a Diverse America* (New York: Amacom, 1994).

11. SAYING EIGHT: I WILL HEAL WITH YOU

150   *I feel sad for many*: David Anderson (@AndersonSpeaks), "I feel sad for many women," Twitter, June 24, 2022, 6:35 p.m., https://twitter.com/AndersonSpeaks/status/1540478786243796994?cxt=HHwWhICx4erS8OAqAAAA.

12. HOW CAN I BECOME A GRACIST?

167 I *commend my previous books*: David A. Anderson, *Letters Across the Divide: Two Friends Explore Racism, Friendship, and Faith* (Grand Rapids, MI: Baker Books, 2001); David A. Anderson, *Multicultural Ministry: Finding Your Church's Unique Rhythm* (Grand Rapids, MI: Zondervan, 2004).

GRACISM GLOBAL ORGANIZATION

Gracism has grown as a global force against racism as Dr. David Anderson aligned his thirty years of helping ministries, governments, nonprofits, and Fortune 500 companies grow in their multicultural effectiveness. The principles found in the first edition of *Gracism: The Art of Inclusion* (2007) have served to transform how hundreds of thousands of everyday people have worked to heal from the cultural division caused by our society's pain-filled racial history.

Gracism Global was established to expand this critical work of cultural bridge building. Now Gracism Global offers training and support to equip leaders to leverage this unique paradigm of multiculturally effective leadership in order to transform their impact. Gracism Global's certification tracks for individuals and organizations guide executives and leadership teams to have the confidence, competency, and connections to lead substantive change in their worlds.

Through convening transformative conversations, the Gracism Global team has served at the epicenter of racial conflict in the United States and around the world. Being called in to mediate for and advise key parties during the peak of civil unrest, the Gracism Global team leads with strategy and dignity as hallmarks of their approach.

As this movement of Gracism grows, you can be a part of it. Gracism Global's resources, services, and team members are here to bring practical and helpful guidance to you on your journey. To find out more about how Gracism Global can serve you and your organization, go to www.gracismglobal.com.